MASSACRE AT BEAR RIVER

FIRST, WORST, FORGOTTEN

MASSACRE AT BEAR RIVER
FIRST, WORST, FORGOTTEN

ROD MILLER

CAXTON PRESS
Caldwell, Idaho
2008

Library of Congress Cataloging-in-Publication Data

Miller, Rod, 1952-
  Massacre at Bear River : first, worst, forgotten / by Rod Miller.
    p. cm.
  Includes bibliographical references and index.
  ISBN 978-0-87004-462-5 (pbk.)
  1. Bear River Massacre, Idaho, 1863. 2. Shoshoni Indians—Wars, 1863-1865. I. Title.
  E83.863.M55 2008
  973.7—dc22
                              2007046560

Lithographed and bound in the United States of America by
CAXTON PRESS
Caldwell, Idaho
176498

DEDICATION

This book is dedicated to Brigham D. Madsen, an appreciated
source of information and inspiration.

TABLE OF CONTENTS

Illustrations

PREFACE

Indian massacres in the West started and finished in essentially the same place: in crimson puddles of blood steaming bright against cold snow.

The book on massacres closed with the most famous—perhaps infamous is the better word—of the Indian massacres, the much-chronicled slaughter at Wounded Knee on December 29, 1890. That massacre gained widespread familiarity largely through Dee Brown's immensely popular 1970 book, *Bury My Heart at Wounded Knee*, a history of relations between whites and Western tribes written primarily from the Indian point of view. Brown's remarkable book (which some historians disparage, but which nevertheless altered the way they do business) tells, in varying levels of detail, the stories of the Navajo, Apache, Ute, Nez Perce, even the tiny Modoc tribe. But he writes mostly of the Cheyenne, Sioux, and other people of the Great Plains.

But there's a gaping hole in Brown's history—and plenty of other histories, which likewise emphasize the Plains Indians—that begs to be filled.

The Shoshoni (or Shoshone), more than any other Western tribe, affected white expansion in the West for both good and ill. These largely forgotten bands scattered across what we now call Wyoming, Utah, Idaho, and Nevada, aided travel and settlement, then hindered travel and settlement, in more encounters and clashes with westering whites than any other Indians, the history books notwithstanding.

Brown, for example, uses the word "Shoshone" only once in his history, mentioning "mercenary Crows and Shoshones" employed as scouts by United States Army General "Three Stars Crook" in "The Battle for the Black Hills" against the Sioux and Cheyenne.[1]

Information on the Shoshoni is similarly scant in many, if not most, other history books.

Despite short shrift by historians, it was the Shoshoni who opened the book of Indian massacres in the West that closed some three decades later at Wounded Knee.

And they opened it as victims of a bloodbath more extreme than that at Wounded Knee, and more deadly than another more famous slaughter at Sand Creek. Worse, too, than Indian killings at the Washita, Camp Grant, or the Marias River.

The Bear River Massacre, on January 29, 1863, claimed 250 Shoshoni lives or more. Brown does mention the incident in one brief paragraph of his book (although it does not merit an entry in the Index), but his description is not accurate. Soldiers, he says, "surrounded a camp of *Paiutes* on Bear River and butchered 278 of them"[2] (emphasis added).

At least Brown mentions it. Some books on the history of Indian wars in the West ignore the fight altogether. A few give it a brief mention; very few cover it at any length. But only one reliable history treats it with detail: *The Shoshoni Frontier and the Bear River Massacre* by Brigham D. Madsen. This ground-breaking historian is responsible, as well, for almost all existing accounts of the Shoshoni, having carefully researched and authored half a dozen books that chronicle the role of the tribe and its various bands in Western history.

This book is less ambitious in scope than Madsen's seminal and pivotal works, confining itself to the story of the massacre and related incidents. It does wander somewhat, laying its foundation on background information about the Shoshoni, and interactions between and among the tribe and the two other major players on the killing field on the banks of the Bear River that day: the military and the Mormons. And it explores what has—and has not—happened since.

But the main story takes place on the day of the massacre, utilizing information and accounts from a variety of sources representing all sides.

It is long past time for the Bear River Massacre to get its due. This book is written in the hope that it will introduce this bloodiest of all Western Indian massacres to a wider audience, while encouraging historians and writers more competent and capable than this author to investigate and report on the event.

❧❧❧❧❧

A few explanations are in order.

"Shoshoni" and "Shoshone" are alternative and acceptable renderings of the collective name of the people at the center of this story. Each name is correctly used by historians, writers, the government, even the tribes, with reasons sometimes given for the choice. "Shoshoni" is used throughout this book, unless in a quotation or proper name which uses the other spelling.

One reason for this choice is simply to follow Brigham D. Madsen's usage. As a former tribal historian and the most ambitious and respected chronicler of the Shoshoni, his choice of spelling is widespread. Just as important, "Shoshoni" forces pronunciation of the final syllable, whereas with "Shoshone," the final syllable is sometimes (and sometimes properly so, as when used as an adjective) seen as a silent "e" and left unsaid.

Many Shoshoni words and names are found in print with various spellings. "Boa Ogoi," for instance, is sometimes "Bia Ogoi." Here, what seem to be the most common variants of Shoshoni words in printed sources are used.

With the exception of "Beaver Creek," which is now "Battle Creek," the modern names of most places are used instead of names which may have been current during the period written about. While Idaho, Nevada, Wyoming, and even Utah did not exist as proper places during some or all of the time described, modern names are used to provide a more straightforward frame of reference for the reader. This applies to cities, towns, and other places as well. Likewise, the Church of Jesus Christ of Latter-day Saints, which is the current proper name, is used throughout in preference to older arrangements.

For simplicity's sake, the names of many of the people who participated in the events described in this book are not used. Those who make only a brief appearance, or play secondary roles, although known, are not always named to avoid confusion. Most of the military officers who led various units of the California Volunteers are unnamed in the narrative, for example, to simplify as much as possible an already confusing and complex incident. Lists of killed and wounded, unit names and numbers, and similar details documented elsewhere, are not included for the same reason.

The work of other writers is quoted freely throughout the text—correspondents, journalists, biographers, historians. But an attempt has been made to use the writings of others in short bursts to maintain the pace of the narrative, rather than including long passages lifted directly from source material. Any change in meaning that may have resulted from the limited context inherent in this technique is unintentional.

Finally, this book is not meant to be an encyclopedic reference for the Bear River Massacre or surrounding events. Those seeking minute detail concerning battlefield tactics, specifics about military arms and ammunition, anthropological and ethnographic descriptions of the minutiae of Indian life, dense facts about Western migration, and such like will be disappointed. That kind of information is available elsewhere. The purpose here is to provide a compelling narrative account of the Bear River Massacre, the historical context underlying the three major players in that event—the Shoshoni, the military, the Mormons—and the interplay among those three groups. Every effort has been made to remain true to accepted facts and to avoid misrepresenting what is known about historic events. The author regrets any failure to achieve what this book sets out to accomplish.

Preface Notes

1. Brown, Dee. *Bury My Heart at Wounded Knee*. New York: Henry Holt and Company, 1970 (Owl Book edition,1991), p. 288
2. Brown, Dee. *Bury My Heart at Wounded Knee*. New York: Henry Holt and Company, 1970 (Owl Book edition,1991), p. 104

ACKNOWLEDGEMENTS

Many people and institutions were instrumental in the preparation of this book. First and foremost is Brigham D. Madsen, an esteemed and acclaimed historian with more knowledge of the Shoshoni, probably, than any other person. His books related to the subject—particularly *The Bear River Massacre and the Shoshoni Frontier, The Northern Shoshoni, The Bannock of Idaho, Chief Pocatello, The Lemhi: Sacajawea's People, Corinne, Glory Hunter*—provided historical context and identified important people and events. His collected papers added additional detail and richness, as well as suggesting other avenues for exploration. His personal assistance provided guidance and wisdom. The author's greatest anxiety is that this book does not measure up to Brigham Madsen's standards.

Newell Hart's book, *The Bear River Massacre*, was an essential source. Mr. Hart collected and transcribed numerous newspaper accounts related to the massacre, as well as military documents, local reminiscences, and correspondence. His collected papers, too, contained much useful material.

Other important information was provided by Patty Timbimboo Madsen, who oversees the library for the Northwestern Band of the Shoshone Nation as part of her many duties as tribal secretary. In addition to generously offering the use of published material in the tribe's possession, she is, personally, a knowledgeable source of information and guidance.

Special collections at the Marriott Library, University of Utah, and the Merrill-Cazier Library, Utah State University, and the research library at the Utah Historical Society house much of the source material consulted for and cited in this book. Besides a wealth of valuable documents, the patient assistance of staff members at each of those places deserves recognition.

The Utah Digital Newspaper Collection, through the Marriott Library, University of Utah, provided convenient on-line access to newspapers of the period, saving hours of reeling through microfilm copies. Another valuable source of information was the web site of the California Military Museum, where transcriptions of many documents related to the California Volunteers are available.

Thanks is also due to Charles Rankin, whose encouragement is the very basis for this book.

Despite the invaluable assistance and best efforts of those mentioned and many others, there are, no doubt mistakes to be found in these pages. The responsibility for all errors is solely with the author of this volume, and apologies are due the sources whose material has been abused as well as to the reader.

INTRODUCTION

As rivers go, the Bear River does not amount to much. The Shoshoni who lived along its course call it *Boa Ogoi*, or "Big River."[1]

In the well-watered East it would not merit such a name. Or even, perhaps, be called a "river." A run, more likely. A creek. Or—most appropriate given the events of January 29, 1863, along its banks—a kill.

But out West, the stream the white men named the Bear is a mighty river and distinctive in its ways.

It is the largest watercourse in North America whose waters never reach an ocean.

It ends less than 100 miles from where it rises, but flows some 500 miles in the trip, draining seven-and-a-half-thousand square miles of mountains and valleys as it goes.

According to the borders drawn on today's maps, the horseshoe shape of the Bear River starts in Utah, flows north across the border into Wyoming, sneaks into Utah again but soon returns to Wyoming, then, in a sweeping left turn, leaves there finally for Idaho and continues its bend back into Utah, never to leave again.

By the time the stream entered the consciousness of white trappers and mountain men early in the second decade of the nineteenth century, the Bear River, the *Boa Ogoi*, and its basins and canyons and mountains and valleys had been among the homelands of the *Newe*—The People—the Shoshoni—for eight centuries, at least. According to Shoshoni historian Mae Timbimboo Parry, they called this part of their homeland *Mo Sa ad Kunie*.[2]

Some 40 or 50 miles as the crow flies, upstream from where

the Bear River empties into the Great Salt Lake, a tiny tributary, whose flow today is occasional, drops onto the river plain and into the Bear on its right bank. On today's maps—those detailed enough to trace such an insignificant watercourse—it is called Battle Creek, in remembrance of the events of January 29, 1863.

Before that, fur trappers, and later settlers, called it Beaver Creek.

At Beaver Creek, and for some distance up- and downstream, the plains rise and the Bear River, over long centuries, cut itself a narrow valley. Curtained by 200-foot-high bluffs on either side, the stream meanders through an irregular mile-wide flood plain. On the right bank, the bluffs are cut and eroded and irregular, with easy access up and down. Above the left bank, however, the bluffs present a formidable obstacle; steeper, fewer cuts and coulees, more difficult to descend or ascend.

A short way to the southwest, less than a mile downstream from the mouth of Beaver Creek, hot springs seep out of the ground and on the coldest days spew plumes of steam into the frigid air. The warm water baths and high bluffs offer comfort and shelter to occupants of the valley from the worst of winter wind and storm, and made this place a popular winter camp for the Shoshoni for longer than anyone can remember.

Among the Shoshoni today, and since January 29, 1863, the place is remembered as an unpopular burial ground. Not a cemetery. Not a graveyard. But a final, uncomfortable resting place for hundreds of their ancestors.

Introduction Notes

1. Letter from Mae Timbimboo Parry to Mr. And Mrs. Newell Hart, April 8, 1976. Newell Hart Papers, Mss 3, Box 29; Marie Eccles-Caine Archive of Intermountain Americana, Merrill-Cazier Library, Utah Sate University.
2. Letter from Mae Timbimboo Parry to Mr. And Mrs. Newell Hart, April 8, 1976. Newell Hart Papers, Mss 3, Box 29; Marie Eccles-Caine Archive of Intermountain Americana, Merrill-Cazier Library, Utah Sate University.

Chapter 1

THE MORMONS AND THE MILITARY

We are invaded by a hostile force, who are evidently assailing us to accomplish our overthrow and destruction. . . . [W]e should not quietly stand still and see those fetters forging around us which are calculated to enslave us in subjection to an unlawful military despotism.— Brigham Young, Governor, Territory of Utah

I found them a community of traitors, murderers, fanatics, and whores. The people publicly rejoice at reverses to our arms, and thank God the American Government is gone, as they term it. . . . I intend to quietly intrench my position, and then say to the Saints of Utah, enough of your treason. — Colonel Patrick Edward Connor, Commander, District of Utah

Mormon relations with the military in nineteenth-century America run a short gamut, from cautious to uncomfortable to hostile.

Almost from the moment the church's founding prophet, Joseph Smith, Jr., reported visitations from heavenly messengers in the 1820s in upper New York state, he attracted the ire of neighbors. Hounded out of New York, Pennsylvania, and Ohio, many of Smith's followers in the Church of Jesus Christ of Latter-day Saints had, by 1833, congregated in western Missouri where their peculiar ways led, eventually, to their first clashes with organized military groups.

1

Through the Prophet Joseph, God named Jackson County and environs as "the land which I have appointed and consecrated for the gathering of the saints," and "that the land should be purchased by the saints. . .that they may obtain it for an everlasting inheritance."[1]

Those who already claimed title to the land did not necessarily agree, and determined to resist both heaven and earth. A July 20, 1833 "Resolution of the old settlers at Independence, Missouri" reported an overwhelming influx of Mormons. "But little more than two years ago, some two or three of these people made their appearance on the Upper Missouri and they now number some 1,200 souls." The Resolution also questioned the character of the Mormons, believing "those communities from which they come, were flooding us with the dregs of their composition."[2]

It is unlikely these new settlers were of a baser sort than the old settlers of Missouri, but they were of a different sort. The roughhewn folks the Mormons found at the edge of the wilderness had arrived there largely from the rural southern states, and carried with them the attitudes of that region. Frontiersmen by nature, they disliked the more settled ways of the Saints, most of whom originated in the towns and villages of New England.

The Mormons, too, were continually experimenting with an un-American kind of communal economy that made the Missourians suspicious. By pooling their resources and importing funds from their brethren in Ohio and other places, the Mormons, though of modest means individually, out-bid the old settlers for property.

Then there were the curious attitudes among the Mormons about Indians. Like most Americans of the day, many Missouri settlers viewed the natives as little more than savages to be put out of the way. But to the Saints, the Indians were among God's elect, declared in Joseph Smith's holy books and revelations to be descendants of ancient Israel, ripe for conversion to the Mormon version of Christianity.

The Missourians also suspected the Mormon interlopers of being soft on slavery. Smith, in fact, prophesied in 1832 that "wars will shortly come to pass, beginning at the rebellion of South Carolina," that "the Southern States shall be divided against the Northern States," and that the "slaves shall rise up against their masters."[3]

Mormon claims of being the one true religion were repugnant to nonbelievers, and that, too, contributed to the persecution of these "deluded fanatics" who were accused of "openly blasphem[ing] the Most High God."[4]

All this, reinforced by fear of growing Mormon political influence, eventually stirred the old settlers of Independence to action. Mobs of unruly men threatened and intimidated the Saints. Violence erupted on occasion. One Mormon leader was stripped, tarred, and feathered; the editor of a Mormon newspaper saw his home and business torn to pieces and strewn about. Afterward, some of those same mobbers showed up at a ferry across the Big Blue River operated by Orrin Porter Rockwell. Destined to become a notorious figure in the annals of Mormon history, young Rockwell was an early convert and a friend to Joseph Smith. Boasting of their deeds in Independence, the men warned him, "Unless you want a taste of the same, you'll chuck the Mormons."[5]

Meanwhile, in Independence, Lieutenant Governor Lilburn Boggs stood amid the mob's rubble. Boggs, destined to become another notorious figure in the annals of Mormon history, reportedly told the Mormons, "You now know what our Jackson boys can do, and you must leave the country."[6]

The Mormons appealed to the Governor for protection, but Boggs and many of Jackson County's leading citizens influenced him otherwise. Mormon appeals to the courts were likewise ineffective.

Through the autumn of 1833, Mormon homes were destroyed, property stolen, men beaten, women and children bullied. Not

3

always willing to turn the other cheek, the Saints killed two Missouri mobbers in a gun battle near Rockwell's ferry on the Big Blue. Four Mormons died and another was wounded in the exchange.

A rumor that Mormons and Indians had Independence surrounded led to the jailing of their leaders. Boggs begged the governor to activate the Jackson County militia and do away with the Saints once and for all. Mormons organized a rescue party to break their brethren out of jail.

The militia and the makeshift Mormon army met on a road outside Independence. The fast-talking militia leader convinced the Saints the prisoners had been released, the danger had passed, and that if they gave up their arms and went home all would be forgotten. The Mormons agreed on condition the mobbers also be disarmed. But the militia leader had no intention of keeping the bargain so it became open season on unarmed Saints, who fled to the relative safety of the northern counties.

Hearing of the rout at his home in Ohio, Joseph Smith demonized Lieutenant Governor Boggs for his role in the affair. "All earth and hell cannot deny that a baser knave, a greater traitor, and a more wholesale butcher, or murderer of mankind ever went untried, unpunished and unhung," Smith said. Rather than hanging for Boggs, the Prophet encouraged "blood for blood, according to the law of heaven."[7]

❈❈❈❈

Joseph Smith did more from the relative safety of Kirtland, Ohio, than sling insults at Boggs. Based on instructions he said came from heaven, he determined to ride to the rescue, and set out to recruit an army.

The revelation called for "five hundred of the strength of my house," but allowed for a lesser number within limits, telling Smith he "shall not go up unto the land of Zion until you have obtained a hundred of the strength of my house to go up with you."[8] As it turned out, Smith was able to cajole 204 of his brethren into service, and the irregularly armed men set out in early May on a mission to save the Missouri Saints.

Despite divine endorsement, the mission was a dismal failure.

The ragtag army slogged through bad weather and muddy roads for much of the thousand-mile journey. Cholera attacked the troops and killed fourteen. Dissension upset the ranks.

By the time the surviving soldier Saints reached western Missouri, their prophet had thought better of armed conflict. Instead, he relayed the Lord's disapproval of the Missouri Mormons' wicked ways, laying a big share of the blame for their difficulties squarely on their own sinful shoulders. "[W]ere it not for the transgressions of my people. . .they might have been redeemed even now. But behold, they have not learned to be obedient to the things I have required at their hands, but are full of all manner of evil,"[9] he recorded in the revelation.

Smith followed the chastisement with encouragement and his blessing, then ordered his troops to about-face and head back to Ohio. A negotiated settlement in Missouri sent the persecuted saints straggling north across the Missouri River to take up residence in Clay County. Some sold their property around Independence, but others, on the advice of Joseph Smith, simply abandoned it.

Jackson County still holds a special place in Mormon lore, and the Saints fully expect to return and build Zion there.

⊱≡❘❙≡⊰≡❘❙≡⊰≡❘❙≡⊱

The anticipated peace in Clay County was short-lived. By the fall of 1836, the few "old settlers" in that area feared the Mormon influx for essentially the same reasons their southern neighbors had. Persecution started anew. The Missouri General Assembly came to the rescue of both parties, this time carving Caldwell County out of sparsely settled territory even farther north, and designating the area a Mormon homeland.

But difficulties continued as Mormons gathered in ever-greater numbers to their divinely assigned and legislatively relocated Zion, and grew more intense as they spilled over into neighboring counties. The Saints, it seemed, suffered from short memories as much as they suffered the harassment of their neighbors. Pious arrogance increased with numbers. Sanctimonious Saints viewed the old settlers as squatters, and promised them eternity in hell even as they squeezed them on earth.

Despite the growing difficulties, by the spring of 1838 Joseph Smith believed Missouri would provide a safer haven for him than Kirtland. In Ohio, a failed bank, real estate speculations gone bad, accusations of fraud by followers, and a host of other financial embarrassments rendered Mormonism's eastern headquarters too hot for the Prophet to handle. He arrived in the Mormon settlement of Far West in Caldwell County in March; out of the Ohio frying pan, but into the Missouri fire.

For most of the next year, Missouri teetered on the brink of war, occasionally falling over the edge in outbursts of bloody violence. It was a confused time, from a military standpoint. Organized vigilante groups—labeled mobs by the Mormons—harassed the Saints. So did officially activated state militia units. One day, an angry Missouri settler might take up arms against the Mormons as an unofficial vigilante or mobber, and do the same the next day as an official, duly sworn militiaman.

The Mormons fought back in equally confusing ways.

Joseph Smith organized volunteer Mormon forces for self-defense. He also had a hand in the formation of an unofficial army to launch pre-emptive attacks against the old settlers. "Danites," they were called. Feared and hated across Missouri, both the fact and fiction that grew up around this secret strike force of "destroying angels" would haunt Mormon history for decades to come. These Danites fought with fists and clubs in an election day battle in Gallatin, then rode out in force after rumored, but nonexistent, marauders in the aftermath.

Arrest warrants were issued for Joseph Smith. Mormons were ordered to move out or suffer the consequences; armed vigilantes assembled to enforce the order.

And still, rumor proved the most damaging weapon.

Both sides in the conflict heard—and reacted to—wild reports of bloodshed and violence. Lilburn Boggs, now governor of the state, activated nearly 3,000 militia troops. Mormon raiders stole a shipment of weapons meant to arm the government soldiers. Boggs retaliated by ordering militia leaders in Daviess and Caldwell counties to do whatever they deemed necessary to put an end to Mormon rebellion.

Hard-riding Missouri mobbers or vigilantes or militiamen—or all three—terrorized the Saints, destroying, burning, stampeding, stealing. Mormons responded in kind, surprising the settlers with their resistance. Three Mormons and one Missouri militia member died in close-quarters combat at Crooked River.

Governor Boggs, by now beside himself because of the Crooked River assault on government soldiers, issued an "extermination order" on October 27, 1838. The document, unique in American history, informed the commander of the state militia that the recent attack placed "the Mormons in the attitude of open and avowed defiance of the laws," and commanded him "to hasten your operations with all possible speed."

Then came the words that made the order infamous in Mormon lore, and forever branded Boggs as, perhaps, the greatest villain in church history: *"The Mormons must be treated as enemies, and must be exterminated or driven from the state."*[10]

The ink was barely dry on Boggs's order when a militia force numbering as many as 250 men blackened their faces and rode into the tiny village of Haun's Mill. Apparently, militia leaders expected an attack from the villagers and determined it safest to launch a pre-emptive strike. A state legislator and militia member said "What we did was in our own defence, and we had the right to."[11]

But no such Mormon attack was in the offing; the folks at Hauns Mill were content to go about their business that day. Only a dozen or so families lived there, but another twenty families were camped out in wagon boxes and tents awaiting safer, more permanent accommodations.

The Saints, shocked and surprised, watched soldiers ride into their midst and commence firing. Shouts of surrender were ignored. Mounted troops shot and slashed at the men, and chased women and children into the woods, wounding at least one woman.

A blacksmith shop served as temporary refuge for three boys— one as young as seven—and fifteen men. The besieged Mormons returned fire with the few guns at hand, but militia members poured barrage after deadly barrage into the wood building, advancing relentlessly until near enough to thrust the barrels of their muskets through gaps in the wall to continue firing.

The blacksmith shop became a blood-soaked shooting gallery, the men and boys inside shot and hacked to death at will. A ten-year-old boy begged for his life, only to have a musket ball blow his brains out at point-blank range.

Then the Missouri militia rode away, leaving in their dust eighteen dead Mormons and about as many more wounded.

❖❖❖

Even as militia troops attacked Haun's Mill, other units of Missouri troops marched on Far West, where some 3,000 to 4,000 Mormons had congregated for safety. Joseph Smith and other leaders there vowed to fight.

The first soldiers to arrive late in the afternoon met a battle line some 300 Saints long. The Missourians opted to withdraw into the woods to await reinforcements.

News from Haun's Mill disheartened Smith. Believing the Mormons at Far West would be treated likewise, he pushed for compromise throughout the next day as he watched the strength of his adversaries reach 2,500.

Militia officers refused to negotiate, demanding instead his surrender.

The prophet and a handful of other leaders gave themselves up as hostages, and spent a long, cold night in the open as their captors taunted and threatened them. Come the morning, they learned their followers must surrender their arms, sign over their property as recompense for their thievery and depredations, and leave the state. As for them, an impromptu court martial sentenced the leaders to die by firing squad in the public square at Far West.

But state militia General Alexander Doniphan refused to carry out the sentence. "It is cold-blooded murder. I will not obey your order," he said, then told his superior, "if you execute those men, I will hold you responsible before an earthly tribunal, so help me God!"[12]

So, instead of being executed, Smith was paraded around the region and displayed before hostile audiences, indicted for numerous crimes, and dumped in a dungeon in the town of Liberty to molder for months, then allowed to escape.

In the meantime, Missouri officials forced the removal of virtually every Mormon settler from the state. Under the leadership of Brigham Young and others, the Saints retreated eastward to Illinois where they would build their next City of God, Nauvoo the Beautiful. Joseph joined them there.

⁂

The Illinois legislature granted a charter for the City of Nauvoo in December, 1840. The document allowed the Saints considerable autonomy so long as they complied with the constitutions of Illinois and the United States. The Mormons leveraged this limited sovereignty to the hilt. Within three years, Nauvoo grew to become the state's largest city save Chicago, and very nearly became a theocracy as virtually every important civic position was filled by a Mormon who also held a leadership position in the church.

As usual, animosity among the "old settlers" grew along with the Mormon presence. Barely established in their new home, the Saints were once again subject to harassment and violence, with threats of expulsion or extermination.

Determined to never again trust the safety of his people to military units controlled by an indifferent, even hostile government, Smith took seriously the opportunity granted in the city charter to establish a militia. Thousands joined the "Nauvoo Legion"—estimates run as high as 5,000[13]—far outstripping any other militia unit in Illinois. Comparative statistics from the time show a United States Army of 8,500 to protect the entirety of the far-flung nation, while the Mormon militia enrolled 3,000 to 5,000 to protect a single city.[14] Smith appointed himself commander of the Nauvoo Legion and awarded himself the lofty rank of Lieutenant General—higher, perhaps, than the rank held by any other American military officer of the day.

Military parades and drills became a favorite pastime in Nauvoo, and Smith himself enjoyed parading around in his resplendent uniform and martial regalia. Some Mormon historians say this was "in part an innocent diversion for Smith, a manifestation of his boyish love of play-acting, games, and entertainment."[15] Following one such day of maneuvers, Smith reportedly said "that his soul was never better satisfied than on this occasion."[16]

The neighbors noticed. "How military these people are becoming! Every thing they say or do seems to breathe the spirit of military tactics," the newspaper in nearby Warsaw reported. "Their *prophet* appears, on all great occasions, in his splendid regimental dress. . . . Truly fighting must be a part of the creed of these Saints!"[17]

In sum with the usual litany of complaints, this strength of arms resulted in increasing unpopularity of Mormons. And now, the heathenish practice of polygamy was added to the list of grievances.

Accusations against Smith of polygamous relationships caused as much agitation and dissension among Mormons as among their neighbors. And despite persistent and insistent denials from the Prophet, rumors continued, even increased. Although few were aware of it—even among Smith's closest associates and family members—his evolving theology had, in fact, grown to include "plurality of wives." A revelation recorded in 1843, but not publicly acknowledged until 1852, formalized a practice Smith had known of—and secretly indulged in—for several years.

By the early summer of 1844, mounting evidence turned some of Smith's steadfast supporters into equally energetic enemies. One—William Law, who had been second counselor to Joseph in the church's ruling first presidency—got up a newspaper with the help of other dissenters. The first, last, and only issue of the *Nauvoo Expositor* published both truth and lies about Mormon leaders and their doings in Nauvoo. It caused enough scandal that Smith, as mayor, had his city council declare the newspaper a nuisance and threat to public safety, then destroyed the press.

As a result, indictments were issued against Smith and his brother Hyrum at the county seat in Carthage. The Prophet outwitted the system by having the courts at Nauvoo issue acquittals. An impatient Governor Thomas Ford ordered the Smith brothers to turn themselves over to the court in Carthage as ordered, and assembled militia units in the area as insurance—both to arrest and protect the Smiths.

Not to be outdone, Smith declared martial law and called out the Nauvoo Legion. He refused to report to Carthage, since neither Ford nor any other authority could guarantee his safety. He then ordered his friend and protector Porter Rockwell to row him and Hyrum across the Mississippi River in the dark of the night.

Forsaken followers sent messengers after their Prophet accusing him of cowardice. Knowing full well death awaited him,

Smith nevertheless asked Rockwell to row the leaky little boat back to Illinois where he surrendered to authorities and was taken to Carthage. Unruly militia units filled the town, with Governor Ford only nominally in control. Then, despite promises to protect the Smiths, he left town and took his authority with him, leaving the most unrestrained militia unit of all—the Carthage Greys—in charge.

As the situation deteriorated, Smith sent word to the officer in charge of his Nauvoo Legion, ordering the troops to march immediately to Carthage. Instead, Major-General Jonathan Dunham ignored his Prophet's hand-written plea, even concealed its existence. The splendid army Smith had paraded through the streets of Nauvoo did not even hear his one and only call to arms.

Late in the afternoon of June 27, 1844, black-faced members of the Carthage militia charged with protecting Joseph and Hyrum Smith instead charged the jail and shot the imprisoned men dead in a brief gunfight.

Despite widespread belief that his church would follow Joseph Smith into the grave, converts continued to pour into Nauvoo. Mormon leaders vied for position, with Brigham Young, president of the church's Quorum of the Twelve Apostles, eventually persuading the majority of members to accept him as the proper successor to the slain prophet.

Raids against the Saints continued. While few dared attack the stronghold of Nauvoo, outlying Mormon settlements and isolated farms were burned and plundered. The Illinois Legislature withdrew Nauvoo's city charter in January, 1845, and with it went the Nauvoo Legion. Non-Mormon militia units in the area made occasional half-hearted attempts to protect Mormon property from mobs, but church leaders soon realized the government of Illinois would do little for their cause. Once again, they laid plans to move on in search of Zion, this time far, far away from their enemies.

Brigham Young, president of the Mormon church, ruled much of the Intermountain West from the day he colonized the Great Basin in 1847 until his death in 1877. Utah's first territorial governor and Indian agent, he was deposed by the federal government in the Utah War of 1857-58. This photograph was made in 1863, the year of the Bear River Massacre.

The search, of course, was not a new one. Joseph Smith had long talked of a great move—Texas, California, Oregon, and Canada were discussed. As early as 1842, Smith had said the Saints would "become a mighty people in the midst of the Rocky Mountains."[18] Smith's prophecy, along with John C. Fremont's reports of his Western explorations, convinced Young and his fellow Apostles that the Great Basin of the Rocky Mountains would be their destination. In February, 1846, the first wagons left Nauvoo, crossed the Mississippi River, and headed west through Iowa.

The move was a massive undertaking, and for the next year and more Mormon exiles were spread from the Mississippi to the Missouri River. Temporary farms and villages were built along the way, and a temporary city established near present-day Omaha, Nebraska, where thousands of Saints huddled through the winter of 1846 and 1847. A pioneer party under Brigham Young left there in early April to establish a Mormon beachhead on the shores of the Great Salt Lake, launching an unprecedented and unrivaled organized migration that lasted more than two decades, eventually populating vast areas of the interior West.

⁂

The Iowa summer of 1846 witnessed a curious encounter between the Mormons and the military. Young had sent emissaries to the federal government seeking aid for his exodus. By happenstance, church official Jesse C. Little met with President James K. Polk within weeks of the declaration of the Mexican War. Little offered—for a price—the services of his churchmen in defending the West. Polk authorized a 500-man Mormon Battalion to fight for the United States Army under the command of Colonel Stephen W. Kearny.

Many—on both sides—saw it as a bargain with the devil.

Many Americans distrusted the Mormons. The Saints' oft-declared wish for political self rule, their continuing efforts to establish an un-American communal economy, their peculiar views concerning Indians, and increasing evidence of the poorly kept secret practice of polygamy made assisting the fleeing Mormons distasteful. Widespread rumors had the Mormons in league with Indian tribes in the West to establish an independent republic and make war on the United States.

Many Mormons likewise mistrusted the federal government and were suspicious of its motives. On more than one occasion the United States had ignored Mormon pleas for protection from hostile neighbors, and some Saints believed the government had even assisted in their persecution. They viewed the move west as an opportunity to get out of the grasp of the United States and establish the Kingdom of God in every respect, including church control of politics. Turning 500 able-bodied men over to the hated government was distasteful on its face, never mind the fact that the men were needed in the migration.

Brigham Young took a more pragmatic view. The Mormons, driven away from prosperous Nauvoo empty-handed, were destitute. Thousands of his people lacked the means to finance a move west. Cash, especially, was in short supply. If the United States Army would *pay* 500 of his followers to go West, he saw that as a bargain. Sweetening the pot was the fact that the government would pay part of the salaries in advance, providing a ready supply of cash for the church. And if supplying a battalion of soldiers would quash rumors of Mormon rebellion, so much the better.

Young spent the first half of July encouraging, even pressuring, Mormon men to volunteer. He promised, among other things, that no fighting would be required of them. The Battalion was raised and Young chose the officers for the expedition.

The Mormon infantry marched out of Council Bluffs on July 20, 1846, and arrived at the Mission of San Diego in California on January 10, 1847, some 2,000 miles later. True to Brigham Young's word, the Battalion never engaged the Mexicans in battle. Violence did visit the expedition along the San Pedro River, when a herd of wild cattle attacked the marchers. Two Mormon soldiers were wounded in the "Battle of the Bulls" before the belligerent bovines retreated, leaving several of their own dead on the field.

Lieutenant Colonel Philip St. George Cooke, a regular Army officer who commanded the Battalion much of the way, reported upon arrival in San Diego that "History may be searched in vain for an equal march of infantry."[19] Most of the soldiers served out their enlistments at various posts in California, and mustered out of the Army on July 16, 1847, just about a week before scouts for the pioneer company of Saints entered Salt Lake Valley for the first time.

⁂

When Brigham Young and his party—143 men (less a handful left behind to operate a Platte River ferry), three women, and two children—survived the plains and prairies and mountains to arrive at Zion's isolated new location he said, "Give us ten years of peace and we will ask no odds of the United States."[20]

They almost made it.

While the Latter-day Saints had left the United States behind, the parting was temporary. The area they settled was in Mexico—at least on paper, for in reality it was beyond the reach and authority of the distant Mexican government. In the isolation, the Mormons intended to establish an independent state, answering neither to the City of Mexico nor Washington D. C.

But in 1848, the Treaty of Guadalupe Hidalgo upset those plans by transferring the Saints' new home from Mexico to the United States. The reluctant, repatriated Americans petitioned for Territorial status, but at the same time established a government for their independent State of Deseret.

This government, wholly controlled by church leaders, claimed sovereignty over a vast area of the West, including virtually all of what are now Utah and Nevada, much of southern Idaho and southwestern Wyoming, the western half of Colorado, a slice of western New Mexico, the northern two-thirds of Arizona, and a large portion of southern California including San Bernardino and San Diego. As a backup strategy, the government of Deseret petitioned the United States Congress for statehood and admission to the Union.

16

Instead, in 1850, Congress lopped off tremendous chunks of the land claimed by the Mormons and created the much smaller Utah Territory.

Tensions between the Territory and the Federal government waxed and waned over the next seven years. In addition to his church duties, Brigham Young served as territorial governor and superintendent of Indian affairs. Many federal appointees sent to Utah clashed with local officials, and reports of bad behavior on the part of Mormons were dispatched regularly to Washington D. C.

Matters came to a head in 1857, exactly ten years to the day of Young's entry into the Valley. A large party of Church members gathered in a cool mountain canyon above the Salt Lake Valley on July 24 to celebrate the anniversary, when Porter Rockwell rode in and interrupted the party.

Rockwell filled a number of assignments for the leaders of the church, ranging from frontier scout to lawman to explorer to messenger to freighter to stockman to—some say—assassin. His arrival in the canyon that day culminated a wild ride from the plains 100 miles east of Fort Laramie. There on an eastbound mail run to Independence, Missouri, he met some westbound Mormons who told him that President James Buchanan had ordered the United States Army to march on Utah.

Based largely on exaggerated reports from former officials— including W. W. Drummond, a judicial appointee the Mormons had driven from the Territory for a variety of misdeeds and dreadful behavior—the recently elected Buchanan felt pressured to act against the Mormons.

Drummond wrote of the Mormons that "no law of Congress is by them considered binding in any manner." And, "there is a set of men, set apart by the order of the Church, to take both the lives and property of persons who may question the authority of the Church." Then, "the records, papers, etc., of the Supreme Court have been destroyed by order of the Church," and, "I also charge

17

Governor Young with constantly interfering with the Federal Courts, directing the grand jury whom to indict and whom to not." Among his many other accusations, Drummond wrote that owing to the intransigence of the Mormons "it is noonday madness and folly to attempt to administer the law in that Territory."[21]

A similar, earlier report came from a former mail contractor. "[T]he civil laws of the Territory are overshadowed by and neutralized by a so-called ecclesiastical organization," W. M. F. Magraw wrote. Lawless conspiracies were "framed in dark corners, promulgated from the stand of the tabernacle or church, and executed at midnight or upon the highways by an organized band of bravos and assassins."[22]

Besides accusations leveled by angry federal appointees, there were other reasons—be they good or bad—for Buchanan's actions.

The Saints had, five years earlier, publicly acknowledged for the first time the practice of polygamy. Then there were ongoing Mormon attempts to isolate their economy from the world through cooperative and collective endeavors, coupled with concerted efforts to keep capitalistic, competitive "Gentile" businesses from gaining a foothold in the Territory.

And, as always, the Mormons were suspected of forming alliances with Indians, stirring them up to harass emigrants along the overland trails that passed near and through Utah. There were also persistent accusations of bands of "white Indians"—disguised Mormons—attacking travelers.

Rather than quietly investigating the situation in far-off Utah, Buchanan opted to act decisively—or rashly, as the case may be. He dismissed Brigham Young as governor and appointed one Alfred Cumming in his stead. Then the president ordered the Army to mount an expedition to escort Cumming to Utah, see to his taking office, and bring the rebellious Saints under the authority of the government.

In his haste, he neglected to inform Young or anyone else in authority in Utah of his actions.

So it is no surprise, perhaps, that the Mormon leader bristled when Rockwell confirmed the rumored approach of the Army. Young wrote to the "Citizens of Utah" in September, 1857, that "We are invaded by a hostile force, who are evidently assailing us to accomplish our overthrow and destruction." Proclaiming the Saints' innocence, he said "We have had no privilege or opportunity to defend ourselves from the false, foul and unjust aspersions against us before the nation." Refusing to recognize the legitimacy of the approaching Army, Young said his people were "forced to an issue with an armed mercenary mob," which "compels us to resort to the great first law of self-preservation, and stand in our own defense."[23]

Young, deposed as governor but not informed of the fact, used his lost authority to forbid the Army entry into the Territory. He called up the reconstituted Nauvoo Legion to repel the invasion, and declared martial law, outlawing any entry or exit from the Territory without his say-so.

During the weeks between Rockwell's announcement of the army's approach and Young's declaration, Utah was a beehive of activity. Far-flung pioneers from San Bernardino to the south, the Sierra Nevada to the west, and the Salmon River to the north were re-settled closer to Zion's center. Church leaders toured the chain of communities up and down the length of Utah, exhorting Saints to greater faithfulness, stirred up suspicion of outsiders and hatred of the federal government, organized local Mormon militia units, and recruited Indian allies.

Mormon hysteria found its first victims when militiamen and Piede Indians attacked a wagon train of California-bound emigrants. The party, originating mostly in Arkansas, was guilty of little else save passing through country so saturated with fear and paranoia that otherwise ordinary people had turned into zealous fanatics capable of unspeakable acts.

The caravan laid over at Mountain Meadows at the Great Basin's remote southwestern edge, a popular, well-watered stop where travelers rehabilitated themselves and their livestock before braving the deserts ahead.

When direct assaults, sniping, and siege proved ineffective against the entrenched migrants, Mormon militia leaders used lies and deception to disarm the travelers and lure them out of camp to be shot down in cold blood on September 11, 1857. A handful of young children were spared; the remaining men, women, and children—120 or more in number—were slaughtered.

❊▦❚▦❊▦❚▦❊▦❚▦❊▦❚▦❊

Meanwhile, far to the east at the other end of the larger conflict, federal officials had been busy mounting the "Utah Expedition," later re-named "Buchanan's Blunder."

The president laid it all out in a December report to Congress. "I was bound to restore the supremacy of the Constitution and laws within its limits," he said of Utah Territory. General William S. Harney received orders to gather 2,500 troops at Fort Leavenworth, Kansas, and lead them to Utah as escort for the new Territorial officials, Buchanan said, "for their protection, and to act as a posse comitatus, in case of need, in the execution of the laws."[24]

The soldiers had marched west in mid-July. Command passed to Albert Sidney Johnston in August, but the colonel did not join his forces until November. In the interim, the army stretched thin across the plains, with little discipline and less organization.

The Mormons would take advantage.

Brigham Young was determined to keep the Army out of his Territory, and said so to the first soldier to show his face in Great Salt Lake City. Fortunately, given the delicacy of the situation, it was a friendly face: Captain Stewart Van Vliet.

Assistant Quartermaster for the advancing army, Van Vliet knew the Saints from a similar assignment a decade earlier when he outfitted the Mormon Battalion. The Captain arrived at the Mormon president's office on September 7. Although he carried no formal notification for the deposed governor of the reason for the Army's approach, he did say that the government intended to garrison troops in the area. Van Vliet was there to see to their food supplies and acquire materials to construct a fort.

Never mind that Young respected the officer. The nature of the quartermaster's assignment compelled the Mormon leader to send him packing, taking with him word to his superiors that everything the Mormon people had grown or built or raised in their Zion would be put to the match before the United States Army laid a finger on any of it.

Van Vliet rode east to meet the approaching Army.

Members of the Nauvoo Legion weren't far behind.

Pending Johnston's arrival, Colonel Edmund Brooke Alexander assumed authority over the force, but may have done more harm than good as commander. Despite Van Vliet's recommendation to stay put and attempt some accommodation with the Latter-day Saints, he was determined to march on. Young sent the commander a letter promising not to molest the troops if they stayed where they were, but that only angered Alexander.

"[T]hese troops are here by the orders of the President of the United States," he wrote in reply, "and their future movements will depend entirely upon the orders issued by competent military authority."[25] The competency of his authority would soon be called into question.

Scattered across the plains with the troops were herds of livestock as well as supply trains heavy with provisions for the army, freighted west by the firm of Russell, Majors and Waddell. Wishing to cripple the Army without out-and-out battle, Young declared war on cattle, mules, and Murphy wagons.

The first attack, launched by Porter Rockwell and five other militia raiders on September 25 against the pack mules of an infantry camp at Pacific Springs, resulted in failure and embarrassment for the raiders.

Other raids proved more successful. Three nights later, a Mormon rowdy called Wild Bill Hickman burned the wagons of three supply trains and destroyed 500,000 pounds of supplies. A few days later, Rockwell's company burned Fort Supply and Fort Bridger to the ground to prevent their seizure and occupation by the Army. On October 5, Mormon firebrand Lot Smith and his raiders seized three more wagon trains and put them to the torch, destroying more than fifty wagons and tons of foodstuffs and ammunition. Then, based on intelligence provided by Hickman, Smith's and Rockwell's raiders joined forces and rustled a herd of some 1,400 government beef cattle.

Colonel Johnston caught up with his victimized command in November. He ordered the federal troops to give up the march and hunker down near the ashes of burnt-out Fort Bridger for a long, cold winter wait—a hungry winter, courtesy of Brigham Young's war on government foodstuffs and supplies.

During the hiatus, Thomas L. Kane received unofficial permission in Washington to negotiate a settlement. A friend to the Mormons, instrumental in the formation of the Mormon Battalion more than a decade earlier, Kane sailed to California, arrived in Salt Lake City from the west, and through shuttle diplomacy throughout the winter, saved face for all parties in the conflict.

He parleyed a full pardon for Brigham Young and the Mormons, and in exchange the citizens accepted the authority of federal appointee Alfred Cumming as governor of the Territory. Kane also arranged for the governor's peaceful escort to the capital city by Johnston's Army, who would then set up camp in Cedar Valley, forty miles southwest of Salt Lake City. The bivouac, named Camp Floyd, housed the largest concentration of troops anywhere in America until the outbreak of the Civil War.

The Mormons got the best of the Army in the end. When the post was dismantled in 1861, Brigham Young and his followers paid a pittance for government stores, buying up for pennies virtually everything the Army owned there, save arms and ammunition.

But in the interim, between the arrival and departure of the troops, it was an uneasy truce between the Mormons and the military.

While the Mormons acknowledged the authority of federal appointees to govern the Territory, it was a matter of word more than deed. Young and other church leaders continued to rule the people. A parade of federal judges and other officials passed through Utah, some of questionable character, others of demonstrated incompetence. Even those who tried to be fair and even-handed were frustrated by uncooperative and mistrustful Mormons.

Johnston's troops divided their time between riding hither and yon through the territory acting as a police force for the judiciary, and vegetating at Camp Floyd. Occasional military expeditions against Indian tribes in the area offered respite from the monotony. Most of the soldiers, including Johnston, wanted out of Utah. "[A]fter one year in the territory," he said of his sojourn, "the novelty of the sublime magnificence of the valley was gone and it has resolved itself into a huge prison wall."[26]

When the government announced troop reductions at Camp Floyd in 1860, the general was the first to leave, departing for California on March 1. He later resigned his commission and died fighting for the Confederacy. Colonel C. F. Smith replaced Johnston, but he soon transferred to Washington.

Colonel Philip St. George Cooke, known to the Mormons from his days as commander of the Mormon Battalion, supervised the selling off of goods, destroyed what went unsold, then, in late July, 1861, closed the books on Camp Floyd (recently re-christened Fort Crittenden, as its previous namesake, Secretary of War John B. Floyd, had joined the secessionists).

And so ended the presence of the United States Army in Utah Territory for the next year and a half.

Colonel Patrick Edward Connor, Commander, California Volunteers, first visited Salt Lake City in early September, 1862. He made the trip on the sly—at least he thought so—from his temporary headquarters at Fort Ruby in the Nevada desert while his soldiers constructed that post and awaited supplies to overtake them from the west. Hitching a ride on a westbound mail stage, Connor stepped down in the city hoping to locate permanent headquarters for himself and his army.

Despite the secrecy, the Mormons expected the visit, and reported it in the *Deseret News* of September 10, with this notation added at the bottom of the story: "Since penning the above, the Colonel has arrived."[27]

The common assumption among many Mormons was that the Army would be stationed at a rebuilt Camp Floyd. Connor and the Volunteers arrived there in mid-October but only camped there overnight before marching on. The site of the old fort, it seems, did not fit into the Colonel's plans for the Department of Utah.

Born in Ireland in 1820, Patrick Edward Connor came to America as a child. He joined the Army at nineteen and served as a Dragoon at Fort Leavenworth. It's likely Connor learned of the Mormons while there, being within newspaper distance of the Saints' difficulties in Missouri and Illinois. According to Connor's biography, his "view of Mormonism may have been formed long before his residence in California or his later confrontations with the Latter-day Saints in Utah."[28]

Honorably discharged after a five-year hitch, he spent the next year and a half running a grocery store in New York City. Bored with the business, he lit out for Texas and adventure. In July, 1846, at age twenty-five, Connor signed on with the Texas Volunteers to fight in the Mexican War. After his year of service,

Colonel Patrick Edward Connor led an army of California Volunteers to Utah in 1862 to protect overland travel during the Civil War. The Mexican War hero fought Indians mercilessly throughout the Mountain West and Great Plains.

he re-enlisted as a First Lieutenant in the United States Army and earned promotion within six months, leading "Captain Connor's Company" of Texans.[29]

The fiery Irish immigrant fought at Buena Vista in February, 1827, where he was shot in the left hand, forcing resignation in May owing to disability. The battle "marked a turning point" for

Connor. "He had proved he had the courage, the staying power, and the stubborn will to survive a crisis that was dangerous to himself and to those he commanded."[30]

Business ventures and adventures in California occupied the war veteran's next dozen years. Stockton served as his main place of residence as he devoted his energy to construction, waterworks, mining, public service, and politics.

But the military was never far from his thoughts, and he organized a local militia, the Stockton Blues, late in 1855. Drill and discipline were the order of the day, for Connor relished a military parade. His company was recognized as one of California's finest military contingents.

With the outbreak of Civil War, the Lincoln administration issued a call to California for volunteers to protect the Overland Mail route from Fort Laramie on the Wyoming plains to the Carson Valley in Nevada. Connor, at age forty-one, answered the call and received a commission as Colonel of the Third Regiment on September 4, 1861.

Following nine months of gestation, during which soldiers were enlisted, trained, disciplined, supplied, and outfitted, Connor's infantry companies marched east on July 12, 1862. The cavalry followed July 21.

The Regiment crossed the Sierra, reached Fort Churchill on the Carson River in Nevada on August 1, and, twelve days later, struck out across some 250 miles of desert to Ruby Valley to build a fort. Eight hundred men were there by September 1.

Neither Connor nor his troops were pleased with their assignment in the West. Despite knowing what the Army had in mind when calling up the California Volunteers, the hope among the soldiers was to be sent east to fight the rebels. Guarding roads to protect the mails and telegraph lines did not excite the Californians. The men went so far as to pledge $30,000 of their pay to offset the cost of transporting them to Virginia, and Connor wired General Henry Halleck, head of all the Union's armies, with the offer to send his infantry troops east at their own expense. Halleck declined.

It wasn't as if the mail route and adjacent telegraph line were unprotected. While awaiting the arrival of the army from California, the government arranged with Brigham Young for the Utah Militia to handle the assignment east of Salt Lake City.

"You are requested to muster into the service of the United States a company of Utah volunteer cavalry," the April 28 wire from Adjutant-General L. Thomas read, "to arm and equip them immediately and send them East for the protection of the mail and telegraph lines extending from the North Platte river below Independence Rock on the old Mormon pioneer trail to Fort Bridger."[31]

It is worth noting that the federal government asked Brigham Young to raise troops. His only "office" at the time was that of President (with the accompanying titles of prophet, seer, and revelator) of the Church of Jesus Christ of Latter-day Saints. He held no government office or official capacity, elected or appointed. By contrast, when the War Department wanted to raise troops in California, the request went to Governor John G. Downey. But, in Utah Territory, it was the religious leader of the Mormons, rather than Territorial Governor Stephen S. Harding, with whom Washington dealt.

Whether he had the authority or not, Young replied on May 1 that the Utah Militia would provide cavalry troops, saying "the commissioned officers and non-commissioned officers and privates, including teamsters, were mustered in by Chief Justice John F. Kinney" and already in camp.[32]

Young and his people had long been of the opinion that the Nauvoo Legion could handily do the job assigned to the California Volunteers, and their coming to Utah was unnecessary.

The *Deseret News* quoted "a dispatch to the *Age* from Ruby Valley on the 30th inst." that implied agreement in Connor's camp. The report outlines the request of the infantry to fight Confederates, believing foot soldiers unnecessary on the Overland Mail line. Saying "Cavalry is the only efficient arm against Indians" in protecting the route, and since "Brigham Young offers to protect the entire line with 100 men," the report concluded the infantry's presence there was "a mystery."[33]

Absent the opportunity to fight rebels, Colonel Connor had his own ideas about what to do with the troops, which brings us back to his visit to Salt Lake City and his aim in establishing his fort there instead of the former Camp Floyd.

Connor's first order as commander of the Military District of Utah, issued from Fort Churchill back on August 6, hints at his motive. He wrote of "Being credibly informed that there are in this district persons who. . .are endeavoring to destroy and defame the principles and institutions of our government," then warned that "Traitors shall not utter treasonable sentiments in this district with impunity."[34]

His suspicions about Mormons were reinforced during his initial visit to the City of the Saints. "It will be impossible for me to describe what I saw and heard in Salt Lake, so as to make you realize the enormity of Mormonism;" he reported to his superiors in San Francisco on September 14, upon returning to Fort Ruby. "I found them a community of traitors, murderers, fanatics and whores."

Connor questioned Mormon support of the Union war effort, writing they "publicly rejoice at reverses to our arms, and thank God that the American Government is gone, as they term it, while their prophet and bishops preach treason from the pulpits."

His recommended site for garrisoning the troops was chosen primarily to keep an eye on those traitorous religious fanatics. "It is on a plateau about three miles from Salt Lake City," he wrote of the location, "a point which commands the city, and where one thousand troops would be more efficient than three thousand on the other side of the Jordan." Connor said he would, upon approval of

28

the site, "quietly intrench my position, and then say to the Saints of Utah, enough of your treason."[35]

So the soldiers marched into a tense situation, unsure of their reception. Army chaplain John A. Anderson said the Mormon "leaders are represented to be in conclave, meditating upon the question," and "the people were in a high state of expectancy as to what the leaders would do, and what they themselves would be called on to do." A leader of the Mormon Danites, or Destroying Angels, reportedly offered a $500 bet that the California Volunteers would never be allowed to cross the Jordan River. "How much truth there may be in these advices, or how much of the real state of affairs in Salt Lake is exaggerated I know not," Anderson wrote. "[W]hether we are to have a fight or not rests entirely with the Mormon rulers," he said, worried that "A small spark can ignite the powder of a vast magazine."[36]

The Volunteers crossed the Jordan on October 20, 1862 and entered the city without incident. Connor marched the troops to the governor's mansion for an address by Territorial Governor Stephen S. Harding. "I believe the people you have now come amongst will not disturb you if you do not disturb them in their public life and in the honor and peace of their homes," Harding said.[37] The men then marched uphill to build Camp Douglas. With winter almost upon them, they wasted no time.

Among the first things the soldiers built was a newspaper, which became *The Daily Union Vedette*, the first daily in the Territory. The editor set out to defuse the situation between Mormons and "Gentile" soldiers in the newspaper's November 26, 1863 inaugural issue.

"To every rightly constituted mind it has been a source of regret that the relations existing between the mass of the people have not been of either a cordial or amicable nature," he wrote. He decried Mormon opinion that the troops were "enemies and persecutors— that they were but the representatives of a government seeking their destruction and annihilation," and said "all such trash will be our province to attempt to correct."[38]

Still, despite the stated good intentions of the soldiers, their presence overlooking the city—their very presence in the Territory—made the Mormons uncomfortable.

⁂

The antagonistic leaders, Colonel Connor and Brigham Young, butted heads in a number of ways.

Connor insisted on a loyalty oath from any Mormon who wished to sell goods to his army. Young retaliated by forbidding all Saints, save one hand-picked representative from each congregation, from speaking to soldiers, let alone supplying them. Availability and prices of goods for sale to the Camp were determined by a church committee.

Connor accused Young of attempting to weaken his force by influencing the Overland Mail, Post Office, and others to pressure the Army into spreading troops along the mail route, rather than concentrating them in his city.[39]

Despite the tension, the leaders managed to keep the lid on. Many Mormons even expressed admiration for Connor's stern discipline of the soldiers, and for keeping expected clashes to a minimum.

But there were lapses on both sides.

The *Deseret News* reported the capture of three city residents scheming to steal and sell government mules. Two thieves, lacking bail, were "confined in the county jail." The third man, appointed to sell the mules, had "of late taken lodgings there" as well. He was "said to be an experienced dealer of that kind, who sell more stock than they buy."[40]

Military authorities turned over to the civil courts a drunken soldier who rode "furiously through the streets, insulting those he came in contact with." He had shot at three men, missed them all, and assaulted a third citizen before returning to camp.[41]

The Mormon newspaper praised Connor for extending the boundaries of the military reserve. "Some whiskey establishments had begun to take root outside of the former lines," the *Deseret News* reported, "and another institution forbidden by Moses was threatening to grow up in the same quarter luxuriantly." By including the offensive properties within camp boundaries, Connor gained authority to shut them down.[42]

Army forays to punish Shoshoni to the north for raids on emigrants, to rescue hostages, and recover stolen livestock were carried out with varying amounts of cooperation from settlers. For the most part, Connor handled Indian affairs with nary a care for Mormon opinion. In fact, he believed the Mormons guilty of being in league with the tribes—selling them arms, encouraging attacks against travelers, disguising themselves to perpetrate attacks, and trading for plunder from wagon trains.

The *Deseret News* heard of, and decried, such trade. "We expect that unprincipled persons are to be found on every frontier who would purchase from Dick, Tom or Harry if they could only 'get a bargain,'" it reported, "without regard to the color—white, red or black, of the seller." The newspaper said, "There is no apology for such illegal traffic," and if Connor, "in the present expedition...be successful in reaching that bastard class of human...we shall be pleased to acknowledge our obligations."

But the "present expedition" the newspaper referred to had another purpose.

Warrants had been issued "for the arrest of Bear-hunter, Sandpitch and Sagwitch, chiefs of a band of several hundred warriors of Snake [Shoshoni] Indians, now inhabiting Cache Valley." Fearing the warrants could not be issued "without a military force to sustain the officer of the law," the California Volunteers marched northward, where Connor expected to "come up with the red skins about eighty or ninety miles from here on Bear River, and that with ordinary good luck, the volunteers will

31

'wipe them out' if the chiefs named in the writ do not deliver themselves up."

While the newspaper expressed some sympathy for the Shoshoni, it said "When he is determined on robbery and murder he needs looking after." The newspaper did not comment on how he should be looked after. "[A]s we may expect better information shortly, on the return of the Volunteers, we shall defer further remarks."[43]

The "looking after" of the Shoshoni by the military on January 29, 1863 would provide the Mormons plenty of fodder for further remarks.

Chapter One Notes

1. Smith, Joseph. *The Doctrine and Covenants of the Church of Jesus Christ of Latter-day Saints.* Salt Lake City: The Church of Jesus Christ of Latter-day Saints, 1989, pp. 102-103

2. Arrington, Leonard J. and Bitton, Davis. *The Mormon Experience.* Urbana and Chicago: University of Illinois Press, 1992, p. 44

3. Smith, Joseph. *The Doctrine and Covenants of the Church of Jesus Christ of Latter-day Saints.* Salt Lake City: The Church of Jesus Christ of Latter-day Saints, 1989, p. 164

4. Roberts, B. H., editor. *History of the Church of Jesus Christ of Latter-day Saints,* "Propositions of the Mob." Salt Lake City: Church of Jesus Christ of Latter-day Saints, 1957, Volume 1, pp. 397-398.

5. Schindler, Harold. *Orrin Porter Rockwell: Man of God/Son of Thunder.* Salt Lake City: University of Utah Press, Second Edition, 1983, p. 11

6. Schindler, Harold. *Orrin Porter Rockwell: Man of God/Son of Thunder.* Salt Lake City: University of Utah Press, Second Edition, 1983, p. 13

7. Austin, Emily. *Mormonism; or Life Among the Mormons.* Cited in Schindler, Harold. *Orrin Porter Rockwell: Man of God/Son of Thunder.* Salt Lake City: University of Utah Press, Second Edition, 1983, p. 21

8. Smith, Joseph. *The Doctrine and Covenants of the Church of Jesus Christ of Latter-day Saints.* Salt Lake City: The Church of Jesus Christ of Latter-day Saints, 1989, p. 206

9. Smith, Joseph. *The Doctrine and Covenants of the Church of Jesus Christ of Latter-day Saints.* Salt Lake City: The Church of Jesus Christ of Latter-day Saints, 1989, p. 212

10. Cited in LeSueur, Stephen C. *The 1838 Mormon War in Missouri.* Columbia: University of Missouri Press, 1987, pp. 152-153. Also, Schindler, Harold. *Orrin Porter Rockwell: Man of God/Son of Thunder.* Salt Lake City: University of Utah Press, Second Edition, 1983, p. 49. Italics in original.

11. *Missouri Republican,* December 24, 1838. (Cited in LeSueur, Stephen C. *The 1838 Mormon War in Missouri.* Columbia: University of Missouri Press, 1987, pp. 164)

12. Cited in LeSueur, Stephen C. *The 1838 Mormon War in Missouri.* Columbia: University of Missouri Press, 1987, p. 183

13. Ludlow, Daniel H., Editor. *Encyclopedia of Mormonism,* New York: Macmillan Publishing Company, 1992. Flammer, Phillip H. Entry on "Nauvoo Legion," electronic version on www.ldsmedia.com.

14. Quinn, D. Michael. *The Mormon Hierarchy: Origins of Power.* Salt Lake City: Signature Books, 1994. p. 106

15. Arrington, Leonard J. and Bitton, Davis. *The Mormon Experience.* Urbana and Chicago: University of Illinois Press. Second edition, 1992. p. 72

16. Smith, Joseph. *History of the Church.* Salt Lake City: Deseret Book Company, 1948. Vol. 5, p. 3.

17. Warsaw Signal. Warsaw, Illinois. Volume 2, Number 11, July 21, 1841

18. Smith, Joseph. *History of the Church,* vol. 5, p. 85. Cited in Arrington, Leonard J. and Bitton, Davis. *The Mormon Experience.* Urbana and Chicago: University of Illinois Press. Second edition, 1992. p. 95

19. Ludlow, Daniel H., Editor. *Encyclopedia of Mormonism,* New York: Macmillan Publishing Company, 1992. Black, Susan Easton. Entry on "Mormon Battalion," electronic version on www.ldsmedia.com

20. Bancroft, Hubert Howe. *History of Utah, 1540-1886, Volume. XXVI,* San Francisco: The History Company, Publishers, 1889. p. 504

21. Whitney, Orson F. *History of Utah.* Salt Lake City: George Q. Cannon & Sons. 1892. p. 580-582. (Cited in Hance, Irma Watson and Warr, Irene. *Johnston, Connor, and the Mormons: An Outline of Military History in Northern Utah.* Salt Lake City: privately published, 1962. p. 4-6)

22. Whitney, Orson F. *History of Utah.* Salt Lake City: George Q. Cannon & Sons. 1892. (Cited in Hance, Irma Watson and Warr, Irene. *Johnston, Connor, and the Mormons: An Outline of Military History in Northern Utah.* Salt Lake City: privately published, 1962. p. 1-2)

23. Whitney, Orson F. *History of Utah.* Salt Lake City: George Q. Cannon & Sons. 1892. (Cited in Hance, Irma Watson and Warr, Irene. *Johnston, Connor, and the Mormons: An Outline of Military History in Northern Utah.* Salt Lake City: privately published, 1962. p. 10-11)

24. Hafen, LeRoy W. *Documentary Account of the Utah Expedition Vol. 8.* Appendix, p.14. (Cited in Hance, Irma Watson and Warr, Irene. *Johnston, Connor, and the Mormons: An Outline of Military History in Northern Utah.* Salt Lake City: privately published, 1962. p. 8

25. Whitney, Orson F. *History of Utah.* Salt Lake City: George Q. Cannon & Sons. 1892. (Cited in Hance, Irma Watson and Warr, Irene. *Johnston, Connor, and the Mormons: An Outline of Military History in Northern Utah.* Salt Lake City: privately published, 1962. p. 12-13)

26. Roland, Charles. *Albert Sidney Johnston: Soldier of Three Republics.* Austin: University of Texas Press, 1964. p. 236 (Cited in Moorman, Donald R. with Sessions, Gene A. *Camp Floyd and the Mormons: The Utah War.* Salt Lake City: University of Utah Press, 1992, p. 100)

27. *Deseret News*, Salt Lake City, September 10, 1862, p. 5

28. Madsen, Brigham D. *Glory Hunter: A Biography of Patrick Edward Connor.* Salt Lake City: University of Utah Press, 1990, p. 18

29. Madsen, Brigham D. *Glory Hunter: A Biography of Patrick Edward Connor.* Salt Lake City: University of Utah Press, 1990, p. 22

30. Madsen, Brigham D. *Glory Hunter: A Biography of Patrick Edward Connor.* Salt Lake City: University of Utah Press, 1990, p. 24

31. *Utah and the Civil War.* Compiled and edited by Margaret M. Fisher. Salt Lake City: Deseret Book, 1929 (From The Brigham D. Madsen Papers, Ms 671, Box 73, folder 9. Manuscripts Division, J. Willard Marriott Library, University of Utah)

32. *Utah and the Civil War.* Compiled and edited by Margaret M. Fisher. Salt Lake City: Deseret Book, 1929 (From The Brigham D. Madsen Papers, Ms 671, Box 73, folder 9. Manuscripts Division, J. Willard Marriott Library, University of Utah)

33. *Deseret News*, Salt Lake City, October 15, 1862, p. 8

34. *Deseret News*, Salt Lake City, August 20, 1862, p. 5

35. Orton, Richard H. *Records of California Men in the War of the Rebellion, 1861 to 1867*, Sacramento, 1890, p. 508 (Cited in Hance, Irma Watson and Warr, Irene. *Johnston, Connor, and the Mormons: an Outline of Military History in Northern Utah.* Salt Lake City: Privately published, 1962, pp. 39-41)

36. Rogers, Fred B. *Soldiers of the Overland*, San Francisco, 1938, pp. 43-47 (Cited in Hance, Irma Watson and Warr, Irene. *Johnston, Connor, and the Mormons: an Outline of Military History in Northern Utah.* Salt Lake City: Privately published, 1962, pp. 24-26)

37. Rogers, Fred B. *Soldiers of the Overland*, San Francisco, 1938, pp. 43-47 (Cited in Hance, Irma Watson and Warr, Irene. *Johnston, Connor, and the Mormons: an Outline of Military History in Northern Utah.* Salt Lake City: Privately published, 1962, p. 28)

38. *Union Vedette*, Salt Lake City, November 26, 1863 (Cited in Cited in Hance, Irma Watson and Warr, Irene. *Johnston, Connor, and the Mormons: an Outline of Military History in Northern Utah.* Salt Lake City: Privately published, 1962, p. 32)

39. Madsen, Brigham D. *Glory Hunter: A Biography of Patrick Edward Connor.* Salt Lake City: University of Utah Press, 1990, p. 74

40. *Deseret News*, Salt Lake City, December 24, 1862, p. 5

41. *Deseret News*, Salt Lake City, January 28, 1863, p. 1

42. *Deseret News*, Salt Lake City, January 7, 1863, p. 8

43. *Deseret News*, Salt Lake City, January 28, 1863, p. 4

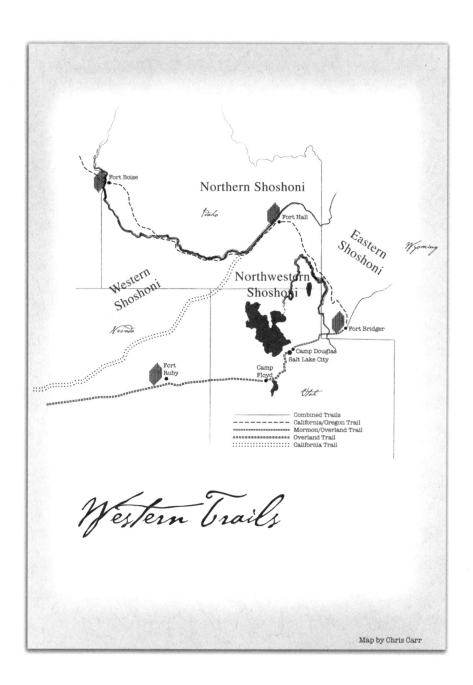

Western Trails

Map by Chris Carr

Chapter Two
THE MILITARY AND THE SHOSHONI

From South Pass to the Sink of the Humboldt, some eight hundred miles, many places favor an ambuscade[;] so many that an enormous army would be required to guard them and patrol the country.— Deseret News, *December 21, 1859*

[I]f there was Indian trouble, all Indians were the perpetrators. Whether the problem was caused by one Indian or two, the whole band—men, women, and children—were guilty by association.
— Mae Parry, Shoshoni Historian

I t was on a summer Sunday morning near the top of the continent that Meriwether Lewis saw his first Shoshoni horseman.

"I discovered an Indian on horse back about two miles distant coming down the plain toward us," he wrote in his journal entry for August 11, 1805. "With my glass I discovered from his dress that he was of a different nation from any that we had yet seen, and was satisfied of his being a Sosone." That record, no doubt, tells of the first encounter between a Shoshoni warrior and the United States Army.

Captain Lewis said the man had "a bow and a quiver of arrows, and was mounted on an eligant horse without a saddle."[1] And while he was pleased to see the rider, it was the horse that delighted the explorer. Lewis and his co-commander in the Corps of Discovery, Captain (formally commissioned a second lieutenant) William

Clark, first learned of the Shoshoni, or Snakes, during their layover the previous winter among the Mandan. From those people and the Minnetarees—whose knowledge extended farther west—the officers heard of vast Shoshoni horse herds, and that they would need some of those horses to cross the mountains.

When the Corps started upriver from the Mandan villages on April 7, 1805, among the party was "Charbonneau and his *Indian Squar* to act as an Interpreter & interpretess for the snake Indians."[2] The "Squar," sixteen-year-old Sacajawea—a captive stolen away from her Shoshoni homeland as a child—would, Lewis hoped, help them acquire horses from her people.

His prospects dimmed during this first encounter, however. Despite all efforts to lure the rider into conversation, when Lewis got near, the Shoshoni retreated, "and with him vanished all my hopes of obtaining horses for the preasant."[3]

All was not lost. Two days later, the Corpsmen "saw two women, a man and some dogs," followed their trail until encountering more Shoshoni women and girls, and bought their trust with tempting trinkets. A little farther along the trail, they "met a party of about 60 warriors mounted on excellent horses who came in nearly full speed." Their intentions were peaceful, Lewis wrote, and the warriors repeatedly embraced the soldiers, "putting their left arm over you[r] right shoulder clasping your back, while they apply their left cheek to yours." Soon, he said, he was "besmeared with their grease and paint till I was heartily tired of the national hug."[4]

The well-known story continues with the arrival of Sacajawea and the discovery that her long-lost brother was now a leader of the band. The Corps, with her assistance, successfully negotiated for mounts and pack animals and guides to cross the mountains.

On September 1, 1805, the soldiers rode away. There would be no other significant contact between the Shoshoni and the United States Army for a half century.

The divisions in the Shoshoni nation in the mid-1800s are perhaps most easily understood if compared to the political geography of America. The analogy is imperfect, as Shoshoni notions of civics, governance, organization, and authority bore little resemblance to those that came west with white migration. Still, it gives some means by which to grasp the basic structure of the far-flung tribe.

Imagine, then, the "Shoshoni" as a nation, like the United States of America, with an estimated population of some 17,000 people. Geographically, using today's maps, this nation spread from around South Pass in the east to central Nevada and southwestern Idaho in the west. From the Wind River Range, the Salmon River, and continental divide on the north, the Shoshoni nation stretched southward to form a southern boundary from—roughly—Fort Bridger to the Great Salt Lake's eastern shores to Nevada's Ruby Valley and westward along the Humboldt River.

Within the nation were three Shoshoni "states," the Eastern, Northern, and Western.

The Eastern Shoshoni, some 2,000 of them, lived in several bands under the general leadership of Washakie. Rich in horses, living amid buffalo aplenty, the ways of these Shoshoni had much in common with the Plains cultures farther east and across the divide.

At the other extreme of the nation, the Western Shoshoni congregated in eleven major bands and shared much of their territory with a dozen bands of Northern Paiute. Together, they scratched a hard living out of a dry land, surviving on plants and small animals in an ever-shifting seasonal engagement with nature. The Western Shoshoni, along with other Indians of the deserts of the Great Basin, shared a derogatory epithet bestowed on them by the earliest white explorers: "Diggers."

In the middle of Shoshoni country lived the people most involved in this story. Four "counties" divide this Northern Shoshoni state. The homelands of the Boise and Bruneau Shoshoni lay on the western border. The Lemhi Shoshoni lived in the mountains and valleys surrounding the Salmon River in Idaho's high country. The Fort Hall Shoshoni ranged along southern Idaho's Snake River plain with their Northern Paiute neighbors, the Bannock.

And, finally, the Northwestern Shoshoni populated the valleys that hugged the Wasatch mountains from the site of Salt Lake City northward to the Malad Valley, the Promontory Mountain area north of the Great Salt Lake, and—across the mountains to the east—the Cache and Bear River valleys of northern Utah and southern Idaho.

Some ten villages of Northwestern Shoshoni people shared the land, under leaders including Lehi, Pocatello, Sanpitch, and Sagwitch. All looked to Bear Hunter as common leader of the several bands—analogous, perhaps, in our imperfect comparison, to the governor.[5]

Culturally, the Northwestern Shoshoni way of life mingled elements of the plains and desert tribes. Horses were important, buffalo and other big game were hunted regularly. Fish, roots, bulbs, seeds, piñyon nuts, berries, and other naturally growing foods were likewise important, and served as triggers to move villages seasonally to follow the harvests.

⚬▤⚬▤⚬▤⚬▤⚬

Located as they were, and as they had been for hundreds of years, it was inevitable that the Shoshoni nation would bear the brunt of westward expansion spurred by the fever of Manifest Destiny.

Trappers frequented Cache Valley as early as 1826, working its streams and gathering there for Rendezvous, a presence which "inevitably disorganized native activities at an early time."[6]

Later, as the westward migration really took hold, the busiest network of westbound trails and roads from the 1830s until and including the transcontinental railroad traveled paths already well trodden by Shoshoni feet.

The Oregon Trail entered Shoshoni country at South Pass, and its various routes passed through the homelands of several Shoshoni bands until reaching Fort Boise. The California Trail followed the same routes for much of the way, with the main trail branching off west of Fort Hall to follow the Raft River southward to the Humboldt River and on to the Sierra. California Trail cutoffs crossed other Shoshoni lands, including the Hastings Cutoff across Utah's Wasatch Mountains and the Great Salt Lake Desert. Other "shortcut" routes embroidered northern Utah.

Like other westbound roads, the much-traveled Mormon Trail entered Shoshoni lands at South Pass. But, unlike other trails which passed through, the Mormon road terminated in the Salt Lake Valley on the southern fringe of Shoshoni homelands. The valley was essentially unoccupied when the Saints arrived in 1847. Although used with some regularity by the Shoshoni, Ute, Paiute, and Gosiute, the area served primarily as a buffer zone in the midst of the tribes. But Mormon settlement soon spread beyond Salt Lake Valley, and the pioneers who went north occupied patches of Shoshoni lands all the way to the Salmon River.

Later incursions through Shoshoni territory included the Overland Trail, busy with California-bound freight wagons as well as east- and westbound mail, express, and stagecoach traffic. The Pony Express Trail followed a nearly identical route. Not all travel was east and west, however—a busy road found its way northward from Salt Lake City to supply the Montana mining district centering on Bannack.

The first transcontinental telegraph line, completed in Salt Lake City in 1861, snaked through the southern reaches of Shoshoni country as it followed, more or less, the Overland Trail. The transcontinental railroad also transected Shoshoni territory farther north. In fact, the final spike was driven in 1869 at Promontory Summit, an area long occupied by seasonal villages of the Northwestern Shoshoni.

All this traffic and settlement unavoidably upset the Shoshoni way of life. Settlers and travelers killed game animals or scared them away, diminishing a traditional Shoshoni food source. Seeds grew scarce as cattle herds grazed and trampled the grasses from which they were harvested. Fish, wild plants, roots, nuts, and berries also found their way into the diets of immigrants, lessening their availability to the Shoshoni who had relied on their bounty for centuries.

Predictably, the Shoshoni were uncomfortable with increasing numbers of whites passing through and taking up residence on their traditional homelands. And the situation only grew worse as encroachment increased. Clashes were all but certain.

And, just as certain in American history, when whites and Indians clash, the military won't be long arriving on the scene.

❖▦❖▦❖▦❖▦❖

The legendary wagon train attack is well documented in Western art, in movies and television dramas, in books, and other iconic representations of the Old West. In the usual depiction, emigrants scramble the wagons into a circle as hard-riding Indians sweep over the horizon, launching arrows into the fortress in the face of withering gunfire. The locale is usually a Midwestern prairie; the attackers are one or another—or a generic amalgam—of the Plains tribes.

The reality was much different.

In the first place, attacks were relatively rare and the resulting deaths few and far between. Illness and accidents took exponentially more lives on the way West than Indian assaults. More travelers were killed by accidental gunshot wounds than by hostile natives.

And there are differences in the details as well as the generality.

Careful research into the peak years of overland emigration, 1840 through 1860, shows that of more than 300,000 white travelers, only 362 were killed by Indians. Very few were killed by the celebrated tribes of the Great Plains. "Approximately 90 percent of all emigrant killings took place west of South Pass," according to the research, "principally along the Snake and Humboldt Rivers and along the Applegate Trail."[7]

In other words, the vast majority of clashes and killings between native tribes and westbound settlers occurred in the heart of the Shoshoni homelands.

The prototypical wagon-train attack, then, was not launched on a sea of grass by Sioux warriors streaked with paint. Rather, it was bands of Shoshoni—disrespectfully denominated "Diggers"—attacking out of sagebrush and sand, rocks and river bottoms.

Romanticized notions of strikes on wagon trains almost always seem to end with the cavalry riding over the hill to drive off the assailants and save the besieged emigrants.

In reality, the cavalry was a long time arriving in the land of the Shoshoni.

The reasons are many. In the early days of western migration, it was simply a matter of a near-total lack of military presence in the West. Early exploratory parties, such as Lewis and Clark and their Corps of Discovery, and those led by Zebulon Pike a few years later, and Stephen H. Long in 1818, came and went.

Army explorer John Charles Frémont and his troops traveled the West extensively, including forays into Shoshoni territory, beginning in 1842. By 1846, with western migration well underway and war with Mexico looming, "the only American military presence in the Far West [was] Frémont and his band of 60 armed explorers."[8]

After the Mexican War, a few troops were left scattered across the newly acquired western deserts, primarily in the far southwest, and in California. Other than occasional mapping and topographical and supply expeditions, it would not be until the Utah War of 1857 that significant numbers of United States soldiers would find their way to the interior Mountain West and Great Basin. In fact, an 1845 force of 250 dragoons led by Colonel Stephen Watts Kearney, initiated with the intention of intimidating Indians into letting emigrants pass safely, traveled no farther west than South Pass.

Another reason for the late arrival of troops in Shoshoni country may have been political. Outsized portions of Shoshoni Territory lay in the vast area whites called Oregon. Other Shoshoni homelands came under United States jurisdiction with the 1848 Treaty of Guadalupe Hidalgo at the close of the war with Mexico. Oregon organized as a Territory in 1849, and "all at once the Northern Shoshoni were wards of the American Government, although that fact was kept secret from them for many years."[9] Oregon's providing for its new wards, or exercising any kind of control or discipline over the region and its inhabitants, would have been nearly impossible given the distance to governmental headquarters in Oregon City.

Further barriers to effective white governance over the Shoshoni were erected with the formation of Washington Territory in 1853. The new political subdivision included what would become Idaho, which included most of the Northern Shoshoni homelands. The new seat of government in Olympia was more distant than ever. Still, governmental responsibility for administering much of the Shoshoni nation officially resided there until the formation of Idaho Territory in 1863.

The formation of Utah Territory in 1850 might have simplified the problem, but, instead, complicated the situation. The imaginary line defining the border between Utah and the Oregon Territory, and, later, Washington Territory, and, still later, Idaho Territory— the forty-second parallel, northern limit of pre-war Mexico— meant that Utah's Territorial government could not officially deal with Shoshoni bands north of that line. This, despite the fact that Salt Lake City was much closer than any of the other assigned seats of government.

Nevertheless, geography—as found on the land, rather than on maps—dictated that whatever attention the Shoshoni in the border regions received from the United States Government in those days originated in Salt Lake City. Besides, Utah's northern border was a fuzzy one at the time; its actual location unknown. Mormon communities in much of what is now southeastern Idaho—including the northern reaches of the Bear Lake, Cache, and Malad valleys—were believed by most of their residents to lie in Utah until well into the 1870s, when a reliable survey finally defined the boundary.[10]

And so it was that military retaliation for Shoshoni harassment of wagon trains, when it finally came, came from the south.

⁂

Billeted forty miles southwest of Salt Lake City along the Overland Trail in 1858 and 1859 were more United States soldiers than could be found in any other one place across the depth and breadth of America.

Camp Floyd, sprawling across the dusty floor of Cedar Valley, represented the tag end of the much-maligned "Utah Expedition," "Utah War," or "Buchanan's Blunder," meant to exert federal control over the reputedly rebellious Mormons of Utah Territory. The Army, under the command of General Albert Sidney Johnston, took up residence in the valley July 6, 1858, and immediately busied itself with construction of the fort so as to complete as much as possible before the onset of winter.

Indian difficulties interfered with Johnston's building program. Utes harassed Mormon settlements to the east and south. Paiute and Shoshoni raiders upset mail delivery and travel on both the California and Overland Trails. Johnston dispatched troops as he saw fit and felt able. He suggested that the mail contractor discontinue service until spring, but was ignored. Later, Johnston sent 150 troopers to establish a temporary post from which to patrol the road between the headwaters of the Humboldt River and the Goose Creek Mountains, but the soldiers found no Indians and returned to Camp Douglas in the fall when emigration ended for the year.

The section of the trail abandoned by the soldiers in the fall of 1858 was the site of bloody violence the next summer. The *Valley Tan* reported an Indian attack on emigrants near the Goose Creek mountains, on the California road in northwestern Utah, with "some five or more men and two women killed." Suspicions arose when some Shoshoni came trading in Box Elder in early August with "mules, oxen, and other articles, unusual for Indians to have." Governor Cumming asked Johnston to send out troopers "to arrest the murderers, if possible, and for the protection of others on the road."[11]

The commander of Camp Floyd complied, but not before exerting his own military influence and stirring the political pot when he "bluntly reminded the governor that he had no authority to call for troops."[12]

Johnston put Lieutenant Ebenezer Gay at the head of two companies of dragoons, and sent the detail north to Brigham City (the "Box Elder" of the news report) to investigate and retaliate. There, Gay learned of a large Shoshoni camp across the Wasatch Mountains in Cache Valley, and was told the village included the guilty parties in the Goose Creek killings.

Gay and forty-two dragoons headed up Sardine Canyon in the dead of night, hoping to make it through the mountains and attack the Shoshoni at dawn. The Indians, however, were not in Cache Valley but were camped in the canyon, where the soldiers stumbled upon them in pre-dawn darkness. Surprised fighters on both sides of the battle attacked and counterattacked, an estimated 100 Shoshoni scrambling up the mountainsides while the soldiers entrenched along the roadside. Come the dawn, the Shoshoni decamped for Cache Valley.

The Camp Floyd detachment claimed twenty Shoshoni killed or wounded, with six casualties among the soldiers. The army gathered twenty Indian horses—one said to have belonged to the massacred emigrants—and retreated down the opposite side of the canyon from the Shoshoni, arriving back in Brigham City from the east with the sunrise. While the army regrouped there, a local Indian who had worked for years as a cowboy for a Mormon stockman was shot out of the saddle—killed by a zealous soldier.[13]

Riding north a few miles in anticipation of meeting up with another detachment of soldiers at the Bear River ferry, the lieutenant again heard of an encampment of Shoshoni and Bannocks across the divide in Cache Valley—this one primed for attack. He immediately sent a courier south to Camp Floyd for reinforcements. Patrolling army scouts happened upon—and took hostage—Shoshoni Chief Pocatello. The Indian leader denied any knowledge of a hostile camp in Cache Valley and claimed he was innocent of any murder or plunder of emigrants.

Believing his prisoner a liar, Gay held him captive and sent a patrol farther north in the Malad Valley and turned up a small village of Pocatello's people. An attack was ordered, but despite all the tactics he could think to try, Gay was outsmarted and outmaneuvered by the Shoshoni, and the entire village—warriors, women, children, old folks, dogs, and horses—escaped.

Gay's troopers set up camp at the Bear River ferry and waited there for the requested reinforcements and the coming of Major Isaac Lynde, who had been patrolling the California road since mid-June. Upon arrival, the major reorganized the combined force, now 400 strong, into the "Bear River Expedition." He also released the captive Pocatello for lack of evidence, and for fear that his continued imprisonment would unnecessarily stir up the Shoshoni.

47

While Lynde and Gay laid plans at the Bear River ferry for troop movements for their Bear River Expedition, an emigrant party from Iowa arrived at a California Trail way station on Marsh Creek operated by a man named Porter. The outfit re-supplied and drove on.

As reported in the *Valley Tan*, the train was "attacked by a band of Shoshones near Mr. P's trading post, and one man killed, and three more seriously wounded—one of the wounded probably being dead ere this." The Indians stopped at the trading post shortly after the wagon train pulled out. "Mr. P stated that he was visited by a chief of the Shoshone tribe, and ordered to leave the country within three days," the newspaper said, "which he did, traveling night and day, and saved all his stock."[14]

The shot-up wagon train made it back to the station while Porter packed up, and he took the wounded travelers with him and lit out northward toward Fort Hall. But the refugees didn't make it. Instead, Major Lynde and his soldiers found them, gathered them up along with the rest of the emigrants who had forted up at Porter's trading post, and took the lot of them south to Salt Lake City, under escort of the entire strength of the Bear River Expedition.

The soldiers then rode on to Camp Floyd, drawing the curtain on the year's maneuvers against the northern tribes.

<hr />

Stirring up dust around the whole problem of predation on the trails through the Great Basin were persistent rumors and reports that many of the Indians attacking travelers were counterfeit—not Indians at all, but white men in disguise.

Reports of these "White Indians" were as old as the Oregon Trail and westward migration. Marcus Whitman, one of the earliest emigrants, told of "desperate white men and mongrels" who, in company with Indians, attacked travelers. The glut of Argonauts rushing for California—with many returning disappointed—

resulted in a similar abundance of depredations. Some travelers posted guards "not so much because of Indians but because of thievish whites." The 1857 Mountain Meadows Massacre, a murderous affair carried out by Mormons (many disguised as Indians) and Indian allies, intensified suspicions that the Saints either engineered or accomplished the suspect incidents. But Mormon travelers were not immune to attack, and Brigham Young wrote of "white highwaymen, painted and disguised as Indians" and warned emigrants to beware. A hostile "tribe of Indians who have blue eyes and light hair, who wear whiskers and speak good English" would be among the targets of army patrols in 1860.[15]

The only thing certain about the White Indian phenomenon is that it lasted as long as the emigrant period. And we can safely conclude that at least some emigrant attacks on the trails between South Pass and the western rim of the Great Basin attributed to the Shoshoni were the work of renegade whites.

What is uncertain, given a lack of captured, killed, or arrested White Indians is who, exactly, they were.

⁂

General Johnston launched an assault on the War Department over the winter and spring of 1859-60, firing off suggestions for an improved Indian policy, more efficient deployment of troops, a re-routing of trails, military escorts for wagon trains, extending the Department of Utah northward to the forty-fourth parallel to include jurisdiction of the most heavily used trails, and reorganization and relocation of the Indian agencies.

Washington disregarded his suggestions. Instead, in General Order Number 10, the federal government effectively "reduced the garrison at Camp Floyd to a handful of untried frontier regulars and relieved General Johnston of his command there." The opinion at the War Department seems to have been that "Camp Floyd existed as a result of the Utah War, which had to do with Mormons and not Indians."[16]

During the run up to the Civil War, Camp Floyd was renamed Fort Crittenden, deactivated, dismantled, sold at auction, and abandoned on July 27, 1861. Relations with the Shoshoni and other area tribes were unceremoniously dropped into the laps of civilian settlers, civil servants, and government officials.

The United States Army would be out of the picture in Utah for the next fifteen months.

⊰▦▦⊰▦⊰▦▦⊰

Despite evolving into the most persistent native menace to westward migration, the Shoshoni were not, historically, warlike. The Lemhi bands in the Salmon River country were, perhaps, the most experienced fighters of the tribe, having for decades fended off the Blackfeet, and, to a lesser extent, the Minataree, Chopunnish, and Crow.

Conversely, the bands frequenting the Grouse Creek and Goose Creek Mountains, who became dogged defenders of their way of life and scarce resources when the California Trail made its way through their fragile homeland, traditionally had no interest in or even any knowledge of fighting. Before white travelers upset their isolation, these people, if threatened, simply faded away into the mountains until the danger passed.

The Fort Hall Shoshoni were experienced fighters, owing to their association with the more warlike Bannock and repeated Blackfeet raids out of the north.

Bands closer to the Bear River—frequenting the Promontory area and Cache Valley—had limited experience with warfare. They sometimes traded raids with the Sioux far to the east, but this more for horse stealing than hostility.[17]

Almost universally, the Shoshoni initially welcomed the whites, from Lewis and Clark who passed through, to the Mormons who stayed. But the overwhelming effects of migration and settlement eventually shifted attitudes.

"The Oregon Trail cut right through Shoshoni land and the people that were moving through there, their stock ate up all the grass that the Indians used for seed to make flour with and soup and mush for the winter, and their stock ate that up," as the Shoshoni tell it. "The emigrants killed all the game that was in the area. So the Indians was getting pushed out of their own home area. That's when they started kind of attacking these wagon trains, stealing stock, cattle, and killing them for food."[18]

Watching fish and game diminish, seeing food-bearing plants eaten and trampled by grazing livestock, the upsetting of traditional migratory routes and seasonal village sites bred desperation and retaliation. Hostility from travelers and settlers, from disrespect to abuse to murder, led to reprisals.

And so, when the United States Army once again rode, marched, and wheeled its way into Shoshoni country in the form of the California Volunteers, it was into a more strained, hostile, antagonistic environment than ever before.

⁂

Colonel Patrick Edward Connor's army of California Volunteers was itching for a fight. The troopers hoped for assignment to Virginia to do battle with secessionists. Instead, they were destined for Utah, to police the Overland Mail route and transcontinental telegraph line to ensure uninterrupted communication between California and the East.

So intent were the soldiers on fighting rebels, however, that they offered to donate their pay to cover the cost of shipping them to the battlefields back east. But the War Department had other ideas and refused the offer. The California Volunteers' only hope, then, was "the possibility of an Indian outbreak along the western trails to test their military skills."[19]

The opportunity would come soon enough.

Connor's expedition pitched its tents on the Nevada desert in September to establish Fort Ruby. Built to garrison troops to patrol the nearby Overland Trail and telegraph lines westward toward Fort Churchill and eastward toward Salt Lake City, the fort was also within reach of the California Trail along the Humboldt River to the north. In the army, Fort Ruby became known as the "Worst Post in the West."[20]

While building Fort Ruby, a request came from Fort Churchill for the Volunteers to investigate the massacre of an emigrant train at Gravelly Ford on the Humboldt and punish the perpetrators. Connor accepted the assignment with enthusiasm and handed the job over to an officer whose name would loom large in the California Volunteers' confrontations with Indians: Major Edward F. McGarry.

The Colonel's orders to the Major were to find the guilty parties, then "immediately hang them, and leave their bodies thus exposed as an example of what evildoers might expect while I command this district." Furthermore, McGarry was to "destroy every male Indian whom you may encounter in the vicinity of the late massacres."[21]

McGarry chronicled his success in an official report dated October 31, 1862. After several days of fruitless searching, three Shoshoni men wandered by and were lured into camp and disarmed. They decided not to stay.

"[T]hey resisted the guard and broke and ran a short distance; they were fired upon by the guard and crippled," McGarry wrote. "Fearing that they would escape, and not wishing to hazard the lives of my men in recapturing them alive, I ordered the guard to fire, and they were killed on the spot."

A few days later, a patrol found "about fourteen or fifteen Indians," and "surrounded them and took from them their arms." Again, the prisoners were not content to stay captured. "Immediately after, the Indians attempted to escape by jumping into the river. They were fired upon and nine of them killed." The survivors seemed content, then, to stay captured.

Over the next several days, patrols rounded up nine other Shoshoni, some of them women and one a child. McGarry released two men, with instructions that if they came back that evening with the "Indians who were engaged in the massacre of emigrants" he would release them. If not, "I would kill all the Indians I held as prisoners in camp." When the messengers had not returned by the next morning, McGarry wrote, "I put to death four of those remaining, and released the squaws and child."[22]

In reporting on "this tragic affair," the *Deseret News* said instructions were followed in every respect save that the Shoshoni "were taken out and shot" by the soldiers. "[T]he order from Colonel Connor was to hang all the Indians that it should be found necessary to execute, but as the Major could not find any trees large enough, he was compelled to carry out the order as stated above."[23]

Whether or not the dead Shoshoni were involved in any killing of emigrants at Gravelly Ford was not known. No one confessed to any such crimes, and McGarry did not allow much time for the guilty parties to turn themselves in—assuming they were still in the area and disposed to do so. Assuming, too, that the captured Indians released to bring them in knew who the guilty parties were or could have contacted them if so inclined.

Nor is it unlikely that the army's ruthless execution of captive Indians had a chilling effect on any cooperative intentions that may have existed among the natives.

In any event, Colonel Connor, Major McGarry, and the California Volunteers had clearly and forcefully set the pattern for their solution to Indian problems, real or perceived.

Between the closing of Camp Floyd in July 1861, and the opening of Camp Douglas in October 1862, Shoshoni raiders, renegades from other tribes, predatory "white Indians" who haunted the roads, or all of the above continued the killings on the emigrant trails. Throughout the 1862 travel season, "starving natives indulged in reckless and almost continuous sorties against unwary pilgrims and gold-miners along the trails."[24] Two of the bloodiest incidents stand out.

Along the Snake River, some sixty miles downstream from Fort Hall, Massacre Rocks earned its name when ten travelers were killed over two days of running battles on August 9 and 10. A month later, an east-bound party bargained with a Shoshoni band near the Raft River for a herd of cattle. Instead, a fight broke out and ten of the white men were killed. "This is reported to have been the fifth or sixth company of emigrants," the *Deseret News* said, "which has been attacked and used up in this vicinity within the last six or eight weeks by the same band, as supposed."[25]

But the California Volunteers' first encounter with the Shoshoni after arriving in Utah did not result from any of these incidents. Rather, it was spurred by a two-year-old affair.

On September 9, 1860, a wagon train was attacked and besieged near Castle Creek, on the Snake River in what now is southwestern Idaho. During the attack, known as the Utter Massacre, various groups of the trapped emigrants tried to break out over the next several days. Most were killed, some captured, others escaped. Among those captured was the boy Reuben Van Ornum.

The boy's uncle, Zachias Van Ornum, spearheaded ongoing efforts over the next two years to find the young captive. When, in 1862, he heard from travelers recently arrived in Oregon that a Shoshoni band in Cache Valley had a white boy in their village, Van Ornum came to investigate. He petitioned Colonel Connor at Camp Douglas for help, and, once again, the commander turned to Major McGarry to deal with the Shoshoni.

The Major located the camp near the Cache Valley burg Providence, and attempted to overwhelm the village by surprise the morning of November 23. But the Shoshoni apparently had been warned of their coming and retreated up a canyon to mount a defense.

Special Collections and Archives, Merrill Library, Utah State University

Soldiers pose with a boy who was the object of an army rescue mission just weeks before the Bear River Massacre. A detachment of California Volunteers freed the boy, thought to be Reuben Van Ornum, who had been taken captive two years earlier following the slaughter of most of his family and several other emigrants. Whether or not the boy rescued from the Shoshoni was Van Ornum is questionable.

Shoshoni chief Bear Hunter and his fighters held off the soldiers for an hour or two, but tired of the battle and called for a truce. McGarry's account says he interrogated Bear Hunter "as to the whereabouts of the white boy, and ascertained that he had been sent away some days before." The Major held the leader and four other men hostage pending return of the boy, and said the chief "dispatched three of his men, and they returned the next day about noon with the boy. I then released Bear Hunter and the four others."[26]

If the boy, aged about ten, was Reuben Van Ornum, he had, in the two years since being captured, forgotten the English language but had become fluent in Shoshoni. The Indians claimed he was "a half-breed, his father a Frenchman, his mother a sister of Washakie, the Shoshone chief."[27]

Casualties, too, were a matter of disagreement. "I killed three and wounded one Indian in the fight," McGarry claimed, "without the loss or scratch of man or horse" among his command.[28] Other reports claimed, "Federal loss, none—redskins the same."[29]

<hr/>

The sweat on the cavalry horses' saddle blankets had barely had time to dry when McGarry once again received orders to engage the Shoshoni.

The soldiers rode north the night of December 4 to recover stock stolen from emigrants, "and to give them a taste of the fighting qualities of the Volunteers should opportunity present" according to newspaper reports. Withholding further comment until the results of the mission were known, the *Deseret News* nonetheless expressed fear "that the northern settlements will not be as safe hereafter as they were before the expedition was sent out to punish them for past offenses."[30]

A week later, the paper reported the return of McGarry's forces, "without having accomplished the object for which the expedition was sent." No livestock was recovered, nor were "the fighting qualities of the Volunteers" demonstrated.

The soldiers located the Shoshoni camp across the river near the Bear River ferry, but were unable to cross with their mounts as the Shoshoni, warned of their approach despite the secrecy of a night march, had cut the ferry rope. Four Shoshoni were captured and held hostage at the ferry, and McGarry informed the Indian camp that they had better return the stolen livestock or the hostages would be killed.

Instead, the Shoshoni rudely rode northward, leaving the frustrated McGarry behind on the opposite riverbank.

"[T]he four Indian prisoners, when the time came for their execution, were tied by their hands in the ferry rope, and in that condition were shot until they were dead." The rope was cut and the bodies dumped into the river, presumably to float downstream to the Great Salt Lake. "It is said that fifty-one shots were fired before life in all of them became extinct," the newspaper told, "which, if so, conclusively proves the executioners were not good marksmen, or that the unfortunate beings who thus suffered were very tenacious of life."[31]

"The aborigines in the vicinity of the northern settlements have, as reported, been very hostile in their demeanor," the same newspaper said in its year-end edition, "since the execution of four Indians who were taken prisoners by Major McGarry's command at the Bear River ferry a few weeks since." While no deaths were described, "the Indians in the vicinity of the northern settlements are mad, and are determined to do as much injury as possible to the white race."[32]

The newspaper failed to mention what seems an obvious connection: the cold-blooded slaughter of bound captives, innocent of any known crime and guilty only of lingering too long at a river crossing, and the ire of the Indians.

But, soon enough, they would be reporting on the "injury" the Shoshoni were determined to do.

Not long after defying the army at Bear River ferry, the Shoshoni band involved likely crossed over the divide into Cache Valley and journeyed north to join other tribesmen. The area where Beaver Creek joined the Bear River, known as *Moson Kahni*, "was a permanent wintering home of the Northwestern Shoshone," owing to protective bluffs, willows, and brush, as well as hot springs and plentiful game.[33]

The Northwestern Shoshoni say other bands would often assemble with them there "for meetings, fun, and games. . . . In early January 1863 one such gathering was held—a Warm Dance. . .to drive out the cold of winter and hasten the warmth of spring."[34]

Not all was fun and games, however. Shoshoni raiders had been engaging settlers and travelers throughout December and continuing into January.

The *Deseret News*, in reporting the deaths of two express agents killed by Indians in mid-December in Marsh Valley, said "that it was the intention of the band to kill every white man they should meet with on the north side of the Bear River."[35] Christmas Eve raids on settlements in Cache Valley and Box Elder won some twenty head of horses for the Shoshoni.[36]

A third bloody incident in early January involved eight Montana miners traveling by wagon, "coming in from the northern mines . . .by way of the new route through Cache Valley," according to the *Deseret News*. Apparently, they missed a ford across the Bear River near Franklin and slogged along the wrong side of the river until seeing the town of Richmond some three miles across the valley on the opposite side of the stream.

Three of the men crossed over for supplies and a guide. In their absence, a group of Shoshoni men "robbed their wagons, drove off their stock, and behaved very discourteously to the five men" left behind. "By some means not stated," the newspaper said, "the Indians were induced to bring back part of the stock."

Come morning, the travelers ferried across the river in their wagon boxes to regain the road on the east side through Richmond, but "the Indians came up on the west bank and fired at them across the river and killed one of the party, named John Smith." According to newspaper reports, the Shoshoni "averred that it was a retaliatory act to avenge the killing of their friends by the soldiers."[37]

As so often happens, one retaliatory act spawns another. But this time, the retaliation would reach unprecedented heights.

The surviving miners traveled on to Salt Lake City, where one of their party, William Bevins, told Chief Justice John F. Kinney about the killing. The judge, not knowing the guilty parties, instead issued arrest warrants for chiefs known to lead bands in the area— Bear Hunter, Sagwitch, and Sanpitch. Kinney turned the warrants over to territorial marshal Isaac L. Gibbs to be served.

"Anticipating. . .that no legal process could be served upon the chiefs named, without a military force to sustain the officer of the law," the marshal, on the advice of the judge, asked the assistance of Colonel Connor at Camp Douglas in making the arrests.[38]

Connor had other plans. According to a special correspondent for the *Daily Alta California* newspaper, the "recent attacks and murders" served as added incentive for Connor to "make clean work of the savages" for "their murderous work for the last fifteen years." So, "Preparations for the expedition were in progress when Marshal Gibbs called upon the Colonel," who "informed the Marshal that he was prepared to start for that place," and "that he might accompany the expedition; but he could promise no prisoners—it was not his intention to have any."[39]

Meanwhile, Shoshoni accounts say that "many of the Northwestern Shoshone were getting restless and concerned" over incidents with the whites. The Warm Dance completed, visiting bands of Shoshoni left the winter camp at *Moson Kahni* on Beaver

Creek in the Bear River bottoms—including the Indians said to be responsible in the recent attacks. "If Colonel Connor had known of the Warm Dance custom, he could have had the opportunity to kill thousands of Indians instead of hundreds,"[40] Shoshoni history claims.

The Colonel armed his California Volunteers for just such an opportunity—each cavalry trooper would ride out of Camp Douglas "with forty (40) rounds of carbine ammunition and thirty (30) rounds of Pistol ammunition." In all, more than 16,000 rounds among the 220 soldiers and their officers.[41]

Those who stayed in the Shoshoni camp "felt that trouble was brewing and could soon break out." They knew that when the whites retaliated, "there was never any inclination to distinguish between the locals and those who came from other bands."

Then, "On the night of January 27, 1863, an older man by the name of Tindup foresaw the calamity that was about to take place. In a dream he saw his people being killed by pony soldiers."[42]

Chapter Two Notes

1. DeVoto, Bernard, editor. *The Journals of Lewis and Clark.* Boston: Houghton Mifflin Company, 1953, p. 185

2. DeVoto, Bernard, editor. *The Journals of Lewis and Clark.* Boston: Houghton Mifflin Company, 1953, p. 93

3. DeVoto, Bernard, editor. *The Journals of Lewis and Clark.* Boston: Houghton Mifflin Company, 1953, p. 186

4. DeVoto, Bernard, editor. *The Journals of Lewis and Clark.* Boston: Houghton Mifflin Company, 1953, pp. 189-191

5. Madsen, Brigham D. *The Shoshoni Frontier and the Bear River Massacre.* Salt Lake City: University of Utah Press, 1985, pp. 3-11

6. Steward, Julian H. *Basin-Plateau Aboriginal Sociopolitical Groups.* Washington: United States Government Printing Office, 1938 (reprint, 1997, The University of Utah Press, Salt Lake City) p. 218

7. Unruh, John David. *The Plains Across: The Overland Emigrants and the Trans-Mississippi West, 1840-1860.* Urbana: University of Illinois Press, 1979, p. 144

8. Wheeler, Keith. *The Old West: The Scouts.* Alexandria: Time-Life Books, 1978, p. 29

9. Madsen, Brigham D. *The Northern Shoshoni.* Caldwell: Caxton Printers, 1980, p. 28

10. Link, Paul K. and Phoenix, E. Chilton. *Rocks, Rails, and Trails.* Pocatello: Idaho Museum of Natural History, 1994, p. 47 (Located at http://imnh.isu.edu/digitalatlas/geog/rrt/part3/chp6/47.htm, July 23, 2006)

11. *Valley Tan,* August 3, 1859, p. 2

12. Moorman, Donald R. and Sessions, Gene A. *Camp Floyd and the Mormons: The Utah War.* Salt Lake City: University of Utah Press, 1992, p. 207

13. Moorman, Donald R. and Sessions, Gene A. *Camp Floyd and the Mormons: The Utah War.* Salt Lake City: University of Utah Press, 1992, p. 208-209

14. *Valley Tan,* September 7, 1859, p. 2

15. Unruh, John D. Jr. *The Plains Across: The Overland Emigrants and the Trans-Mississippi West, 1840-1860.* Urbana: University of Illinois Press, Paperback edition, 1982, pp. 151-153

16. Moorman, Donald R. and Sessions, Gene A. *Camp Floyd and the Mormons: The Utah War.* Salt Lake City: University of Utah Press, 1992, p. 216-219

17. Steward, Julian H. *Basin-Plateau Aboriginal Sociopolitical Groups.* Washington: United States Government Printing Office, 1938 (reprint, 1997, The University of Utah Press, Salt Lake City) pp. 176, 179, 192, 207

18. Ivan Wongan interview, "Northwestern Band of the Shoshone Nation" (video program) Norman: University of Oklahoma American Indian Institute in conjunction with Northwestern Band of the Shoshone Nation, Lewis-Clark State College Educational Technology Department, State of Idaho Department of Health and Welfare. 1992

19. Madsen, Brigham D. *Glory Hunter: A Biography of Patrick Edward Connor.* Salt Lake City: University of Utah Press, 1990, p. 57

20. "Fort Ruby, Ruby Valley, Nevada," White Pine County Historical Society. Record located on the Internet, http://www.webpanda.com/white_pine_county/historical_society/ft_ruby.htm, February 19, 2003

21. Madsen, Brigham D. *Glory Hunter: A Biography of Patrick Edward Connor.* Salt Lake City: University of Utah Press, 1990, p. 61-62

22. Record located on the Internet, http://www.militarymuseum.org/2dCavVC.html. *California State Military Department, "The California Military Museum."* Information "Extracted from *Records of California Men in the War of the Rebellion, 1861 To 1867.*"

23. *Deseret News,* November 19, 1862, p. 4

24. Madsen, Brigham D. *The Shoshoni Frontier and the Bear River Massacre.* Salt Lake City: University of Utah Press, 1985, p. 162

25. *Deseret News,* September 24, 1862, p. 4

26. Record located on the Internet, http://www.militarymuseum.org/2dCavVC.html. *California State Military Department, "The California Military Museum."* Information "Extracted from *Records of California Men in the War of the Rebellion, 1861 To 1867.*"

27. Carter, Kate B., compiler. *Our Pioneer Heritage: Volume Six.* Salt Lake City: Daughters of the Utah Pioneers, 1963, p. 118

28. Record located on the Internet, http://www.militarymuseum.org/2dCavVC.html. *California State Military Department, "The California Military Museum."* Information *"*Extracted from *Records of California Men in the War of the Rebellion, 1861 To 1867."*

29. Carter, Kate B., compiler. *Our Pioneer Heritage: Volume Six.* Salt Lake City: Daughters of the Utah Pioneers, 1963, p. 118

30. *Deseret News*, December 10, 1862, p. 4

31. *Deseret News*, December 17, 1862, p. 5

32. *Deseret News*, December 31, 1862, p. 4

33. Parry, Mae. "Early History" in *Coyote Steals Fire: A Shoshone Tale.* Retold and Illustrated by The Northwestern Band of the Shoshone Nation. Logan: Utah State University Press, 2005

34. Parry, Mae. "The Northwestern Shoshone," in *A History of Utah's American Indians.* Edited by Cuch, Forrest S. Salt Lake City: Utah State Division of Indian Affairs / Utah State Division of History, 2000, p. 33

35. *Deseret News*, January 14, 1863, p. 8

36. Madsen, Brigham D. *The Shoshoni Frontier and the Bear River Massacre.* Salt Lake City: University of Utah Press, 1985, pp. 174-175

37. *Deseret News*, January 21, 1863, p. 5

38. *Deseret News,* January 28, 1863, p. 4

39. Record located on the Internet, http://www.militarymuseum.org/2dCavVC.html. *California State Military Department, "The California Military Museum."* Report on "The Battle of Bear River"

40. Parry, Mae. "The Northwestern Shoshone," in *A History of Utah's American Indians.* Edited by Cuch, Forrest S. Salt Lake City: Utah State Division of Indian Affairs / Utah State Division of History, 2000, pp. 33-34

41. Madsen, Brigham D. *The Shoshoni Frontier and the Bear River Massacre.* Salt Lake City: University of Utah Press, 1985, pp. 180-181

42. Parry, Mae. "The Northwestern Shoshone," in *A History of Utah's American Indians.* Edited by Cuch, Forrest S. Salt Lake City: Utah State Division of Indian Affairs / Utah State Division of History, 2000, pp. 34

Chapter Three
THE SHOSHONI AND THE SAINTS

The scarcity of game in these Territories, and the occupation of the most fertile portions thereof by our settlements, have reduced these Indians to a state of extreme destitution, and for several years past they have been almost literally compelled to resort to plunder in order to obtain the necessaries of life. — James Duane Doty, Superintendent of Indian Affairs, Utah Territory

We have ever pursued this policy toward them to feed and clothe them and then if they presumed upon forbearance to become ugly and saucy and hostile beyond endurance to chastise them. Yet we have never lost sight of this policy to conciliate them as soon as possible. — Brigham Young, President, Church of Jesus Christ of Latter-day Saints

When the Mormons marched westward to Shoshoni territory in 1847, they came armed with attitudes that differed significantly from any other emigrants of the day. These differences, in turn, affected the way American Indians were treated. Policies voiced by Mormon leaders tended to be more cooperative, more accommodating, more supportive of the native people whose lands they passed through or occupied.

But, in the end, the Indians in "Mormon Country" were treated no differently, no better, than other western tribes.

The good intentions of Mormon leaders may have delayed, in Utah, the near-total displacement of Indian cultures by the seemingly irresistible force of white settlement, but the delay was both brief and temporary. Eventually, the same clashes came to define relationships between the Shoshoni and the Saints that described the general course and destination of Indian-white relations throughout the West.

The road by which they arrived at that place in the Mormon Zion, however, included unique twists and turns given Shoshoni attitudes about emigrants and settlers, and Mormon attitudes about Indians. All of which was complicated by the attitudes of the Saints about the United States of America, which they had so recently left, voluntarily, and to which they were involuntarily rejoined.

❖▪❖▪❖▪❖

Early Shoshoni encounters with Americans on the Western trails echoed the earliest encounter with the Lewis and Clark expedition—suspicion, followed by curiosity, resulting in assistance.

Washakie and his Eastern Shoshoni were said to offer "the most consistently praiseworthy Indian assistance." Numerous reports tell of Indians—Shoshoni and others—recovering lost livestock, providing firewood, cutting grass for hay, assisting at river crossings, trading for food or giving it gratis, and selling fresh livestock to replace spent horses and cattle.[1] Indians served as guides, as well, since the emigrant trails seldom, contrary to legend, crossed vast untracked wilderness, but tended instead to adhere to well-worn Indian highways long used for trade and travel.

Mormon emigrants recognized the important role Indians would play in their exodus to the West, even in its earliest stages, slogging across Iowa in 1846. The Saints wanted "the privilege of staying on their land this winter, cutting timber, building houses, perhaps leaving some families and crops," Brigham Young said, "and if they want pay for occupancy of their lands, we will pay them."[2]

Both Shoshoni and Ute traders called upon Mormon pioneers within days of their sowing the first seeds where Salt Lake City would take root and grow. The tribes quarreled with each other over who was on whose land, and who had the right to sell or trade it away.

Young was in his sickbed during the meeting, but Heber C. Kimball spoke for him during and afterward, revealing a different attitude toward occupying Indian lands. "The land belongs to our Father in Heaven, and we calculate to plow and plant it;" Kimball said, "and no man shall have the power to sell his inheritance for he cannot remove it; it belongs to the Lord."[3]

Still, the Mormons intended to coexist with the Indians as much as possible, an intention stemming from a unique view of Indians and their proper place in the world and the West. Indians were believed to be among God's elect, declared in Mormon prophet Joseph Smith's holy books and revelations to be descendants of ancient Israel by way of a series of migrations from the Holy Land in Biblical times, only to degenerate to a fallen condition through sin and iniquity. "Lamanites," they called these remnants of the wicked *Book of Mormon* anti-heroes of the same name.

As early as 1830, within months of the formal organization of his church, the Prophet sent missionaries "into the wilderness among the Lamanites."[4] Once converted, he prophesied, the "Lamanites shall blossom as a rose"[5] in preparation for the second coming of Jesus Christ.

Until that day, the Indians must be embraced. "The sons and daughters of Zion will soon be required to devote a portion of their time in instructing the children of the forest," Mormon Apostle Parley P. Pratt had written in 1845 on behalf of his brethren. "For they must be educated, and instructed in all the arts of civil life, as well as in the gospel." Pratt went on to say that the Indians "must be clothed, fed, and instructed in the principles and practices of virtue" and other qualities consistent with "sons and daughters of the royal house of Israel."[6]

The intended implementation of those ideals in the Great Basin was summarized in practical terms in a now-legendary phrase said to have originated with Brigham Young: "It is cheaper to feed the Indians than fight them."

The settlers would pay a heavy price for the policy in times of scarcity to come. But the price paid by the Shoshoni would be heavier beyond measure.

⁂

For their part, the Shoshoni "believed that a friendly relationship was possible with the pioneers. As a result, the Mormon pioneers and their leaders were initially welcomed in the Shoshone country."[7]

At the outset, at least, the same belief may have applied to travelers passing through. But the killing—of both whites and Indians—increased with increasing activity on the trails. The causes were many. Both Indians and emigrants initiated violence, which often resulted in violent retaliation against the most convenient targets, regardless of guilt or innocence. "Yet even though historical responsibility is by no means onesided," one researcher claims, "the callous attitude of cultural and racial superiority so many overlanders exemplified was of considerable significance in producing the volatile milieu in which more and more tragedies occurred."[8]

For the first decade or so of Mormon settlement, disagreements with Shoshoni bands were few. Shoshoni clashes with whites occurred mostly with travelers on the Oregon and California trails, while the Saints' difficulties with Indians primarily involved the Utes.

But not exclusively.

"Well, in 1847 the Mormons came into the valley and then, from that point on, the Northwestern Band's lifestyle was completely changed. Because the Mormons moved in here, they meant to stay, they weren't just passing through," the Shoshoni remember. "And as they stayed, well then they started farming, they started settlements, and it was more permanent, fencing the land. And, again, the Indians started to get pushed off their land and then they retaliated. . . .by raiding and stealing stock."[9]

An early violent clash between Mormon settlers and the Shoshoni stemmed from an incident of mistaken horse stealing.

As Mormon settlement crept northward, the Saints were soon in uncomfortable proximity to Shoshoni villages along the Weber and Ogden rivers. (The bands were incorrectly called "Weber Utes.") One night in September, 1850, a nervous settler shot and killed Terrikee when he saw the Shoshoni chief taking horses from his cornfield. The shooter thought he had killed a rustler in the act, but Terrikee was fetching his own horses, which had wandered into the farm field.

Fearing reprisal, most of the frightened settlers clustered in town to await aid from Salt Lake City. Angry Indians killed a Mormon man named Campbell, then left the area. Militia forces from Salt Lake City could not find the departed Indians. "It is my opinion that they are satisfied," the militia leader reported up the chain of command. "They have had blood for blood, Campbell for Terrikee, and will return to their tribe contented."[10]

Ongoing difficulties with Ute bands and the scrape with the Shoshoni caused Mormon leaders to question their desire to coexist with the Indians.

One proposed solution was that the federal government quash any Indian claims to territory in Utah and relocate them to "some favorable point on the eastern slope of the Sierra Nevada. . .or to the Wind River chain of mountains," according to a letter to their agent in Washington, D.C. "The progress of civilization, the safety of the mails, and the welfare of the Indians themselves called for the adoption of this policy," the November 20, 1850, letter said.[11]

"We have spared no time and expense in endeavoring to conciliate the Indians, and learn them to leave off their habits of pilfering and plundering and work like other people," Brigham Young said to assembled political leaders on December 2, 1850, upon announcing the federal government's formation of Utah Territory. "Could they be induced to live peacefully and keep herds of cattle, then conditions would very materially be ameliorated, and gradually induce a return to the habits of civilization."[12]

Despite second thoughts such as these about Indian policy, Mormon leaders, for the most part, continued to promote co-existence with area tribes, "feeding rather than fighting." And the previously voiced patronizing opinion that the Indians needed "improving" consistently remained the Mormon point of view.

In a speech before the Utah Territorial Legislature in December, 1854, Brigham Young said, "I have uniformly pursued a friendly course toward them, feeling convinced that independent of the question of exercising humanity towards so degraded and ignorant a race of people, it was manifestly more economical and less expensive to feed and clothe, than fight them."[13]

The same policy held sway as late as 1866. "I wish to impress [all] with the necessity of treating the Indians with kindness, and to refrain from harboring the revengeful, vindictive feeling that many indulge in," Brigham Young sermonized. "Never turn them away hungry from your door, teach them the arts of husbandry, bear with them in all patience and long suffering, and never consider their lives as equivalent for petty stealing."[14]

❖▦❖▦❖▦❖▦❖

Implementing the official Mormon policy was never easy. And it became increasingly difficult as thousands upon thousands of church members and converts poured into the Territory year after year. Settlements were established in every nook and cranny that offered sufficient graze for livestock, terrain and soil suitable to the plow, and a reliable stream that could be diverted for irrigation.

All of these activities, essential to white settlement, were disruptive, if not downright destructive, of the Shoshoni way of life.

Semi-nomadic, the Shoshoni required vast tracts of land and significant travel to keep food coffers filled. "Many Shoshone people traveled in western Wyoming and Utah to hunt buffalo, elk, moose, and pronghorn," according to Shoshoni history. Smaller game and birds, such as rabbits, squirrels, woodchucks, ducks, geese, grouse, and doves were hunted. "During the summer and fall months the Northwestern Shoshone spent their time gathering seeds, roots, and berries for family use. . . .Late summer was root digging time." Pine nuts were gathered in late fall. It was a delicate dance with nature, in which "The mountains, streams, and plains stood forever," the Shoshoni said, "and the seasons walked around annually."[15]

Mormon settlement on traditional Shoshoni homelands meant competition for game animals, fish, and birds. Grass fields were grazed off or cut for hay before seeds could be harvested, ground plowed to yield something other than native bulbs and roots.

Problems all, all of which grew increasingly difficult with the passage of years.

Brigham Young sent settlers far away to the northern limits of Shoshoni homelands in 1855 to help realize his territorial ambitions. By mid June, a mission was established on a branch of the Salmon River. A Snake Indian [Shoshoni] soon reported that "the Mormons are hard at work Sowing wheat planting potatoes etc. etc. etc. and building houses."[16]

Between the Salmon River and earlier settlements on the Weber River, Mormon colonization of lands used by the Shoshoni since before memory included Brigham City (Box Elder) and North Ogden in 1850, Pleasant View and Willard in 1851, and Perry (Porters Spring) in 1853.

A few miles north and east and across the mountains from the main chain of valleys linking the Great Salt Lake and the Wasatch range lies Cache Valley. The Northwestern Shoshoni of the day might have called it the heart of their homelands, and many a winter was spent along the banks of the Bear River at the valley's northern end.

In 1855, Governor Brigham Young and the Territorial government of Utah passed a law giving title to Cache Valley "to Brigham Young, Trustee in the Trust for the Church of Jesus Christ of Latter Day Saints. . .for a herd ground and other purposes."[17] The Shoshoni, as usual, were not consulted concerning this change of title.

The Governor and Trustee-in-Trust wasted no time in putting his newly acquired grazing allotment to good purpose. A crew in mid-July put up corrals, fences, sheds, and houses, nailed a set of antlers over the front gate and called their work the Elkhorn Ranch. Not long after, Brigham Young's cowboys trailed 3,000 head of cattle through the canyon.

The drovers were experienced hands, having herded Mormon cattle in the Promontory area, some fifty miles as the wind blows west of their new home. But nothing prepared them for a Cache Valley winter, where the snows often lay long and deep. The drovers forced as many starving cattle as they could back across the snowbound mountains to the lower-lying Salt Lake Valley. By any tally, the loss of more than 2,000 head that first winter rendered the herd ground a failure.

Despite the dismal experience of the Elkhorn Ranch, Mormon leaders still considered the place ripe for settlement, and in September, 1856, Peter Maughan led the first colonists into Cache Valley and established Maughan's Fort, later Wellsville, in the southwest corner of the basin. "With little regard for Indian patterns of travel, villages, or hunting grounds, the Mormon pioneers began spreading on to new land."[18]

The Northwestern Shoshoni who called the neighborhood home didn't hesitate to call on Maughan's settlement from time to time. Of one such incident, Maughan wrote to Brigham Young that a band of about fifty angry Shoshoni warriors, "all stripped naked ...roade around and yelled like as many fiends" complaining "that we were living on their Land, etc etc." The gift of a cow quelled the protest.[19]

Settlement in Cache Valley and elsewhere in Deseret was interrupted when Brigham Young called all the hived-off colonists back home upon learning that federal troops were on the march to quash a supposed rebellion in Utah Territory. Maughan got the evacuation order in October, 1857, but most of the Cache Valley settlers stayed the winter and sowed crops in early spring. By the end of March, 1858, Wellsville was abandoned. When a negotiated settlement ended the threatened war before it started in earnest and peace settled in, settlers were authorized to return by fall and some did—in time to harvest the crops planted that spring.

Brigham Young's authorization to return to Cache Valley came with a caveat, however. "You are perfectly aware Brother Maughan that you at that place are perfectly cut off from any assistance from any of our settlements during the winter," he wrote in a letter. He warned Maughan it would be necessary to "rely entirely upon your own resources," and that "You must be very cautious about the hostile Indians from the north."[20]

<hr />

Calling home Saints from far-flung settlements had been but one of Brigham Young's many preparations for war with the United States of America in 1857. Some of those plans involved the Shoshoni.

Dimick Huntington, one of Brigham Young's tools in dealing with Indians, recorded an August 30 meeting with several Shoshoni on the Weber River. "I told them that the Lord had come out of his Hiding place & they had to commence their work," he wrote. "I gave them all the Beef Cattle & horses on the Road to California the North rout."[21] It seems Huntington, for and on behalf of Brigham Young, had deeded over to the Shoshoni emigrant cattle to which the Mormons did not hold title.

Further meetings had, or would, occur between Huntington and other Shoshoni bands, as he attempted to trade bread and beef and other foodstuffs for loyalty.

With the United States Army tramping around Washakie's country in November, 1857, Brigham Young thought to write the chief and apprise him of the Saints' side of the situation. In a November 2 letter, the Mormon leader told his Eastern Shoshoni counterpart that the United States intended all manner of evil for his church and people—and that the Shoshoni weren't safe, either. "You know that when the Americans come to you they want to lie with your squaws, but the Mormons do not," he warned.

"Now we don't want to fight them, if they will only go away and not try to abuse and kill us when we try to do right. But if they try to kill us we shall defend ourselves," Young wrote, then told the Indians "we do not want you to fight on the side of those wicked men." The Mormons expected, at the very least, neutrality. "I do not want you to fight the Americans nor to fight us for them, for we can take care ourselves."[22]

For the most part, the widespread Shoshoni bands avoided contact with the approaching army. And, with the negotiated settlement ending hostilities between the soldiers and the Saints, the Indians did not take up arms for or against either party in the dispute.

Among the Mormons—although officially opposed to the establishment of Camp Floyd and the presence of federal troops as peacekeepers—there were widespread expectations that the army would make their settlements safer. They hoped for protection from Indian plunder, wished for security against attacks, and longed for relief from the costly "cheaper to feed than fight them" policy.

The Secretary of War saw Mormon-Indian relations differently.

"All other Territories and people upon our vast frontiers suffer from Indian depredations, but the Mormon people enjoy an immunity from their outrages," John B. Floyd reported to Congress. "For the protection of these people against Indians there is no necessity for the presence of a single soldier."[23]

In the meantime, attacks along the emigrant trails continued. Blame was distributed widely.

Brigham Young said much of the bloodshed was caused by trigger-happy travelers and a lack of government rations for the Shoshoni. He also claimed fear of the soldiers at Camp Floyd contributed to the unrest.

Some government officials blamed the Mormons for encouraging Indian attacks on emigrants and stirring up anti-American (and pro-Mormon) sentiment among the tribes.

Then there were persistent reports and rumors among travelers that many attacks were carried out by white men disguised as Indians—Mormon renegades according to some, depending on loyalties, or desperados operating out of California according to others. Just how much of the "white Indians" stories was rumor and how much was true is impossible to know. Likewise, the dogged gossip that if you scraped the paint off these predators of the trail you'd find a Mormon underneath.

There is no doubt, however, that tales of marauding bands of pale-faced Indians were well known and widespread at the time. One historian of the western trail reports "a substantial amount of evidence" that Indian attacks weren't always the work of Indians. Some observations were "bizarre but persuasive," such as the dying testimony of one westbound woman traveler that the Indians who raped and shot her weren't Indians at all—she observed during the ordeal that her attackers had neglected to paint "the whole body."[24]

Renowned tourist Sir Richard F. Burton visited "The City of the Saints" in 1860, and such stories were still persistent. On the way out of town, he tipped several tumblers of valley tan with Porter Rockwell. When the "old Danite" learned Burton's party planned to travel to California, he offered advice on avoiding Indian trouble on the trail. Rockwell urged Burton, especially, to avoid "'White Indians,' the worst of their kind," by steering clear of the main trail, which, he claimed, the danger made "as fit for traveling as h—ll is for a powder magazine."[25]

At the end of 1858, given ongoing predators on the emigrant trails and continuing clashes between settlers and Shoshoni, the situation was far from stable—even with the Utah War off the table and the supposedly stabilizing presence of federal troops.

Differences of opinion, contrary expectations, and widespread anxiety did not bode well for the future of the Shoshoni in Mormon country, or the security of Mormon settlers on Shoshoni homelands.

⁂

As Mormon converts streamed to their "Promised Land" by the thousands in the years following the Utah War, Cache Valley's fertile soil, plentiful water, and verdant beauty made it attractive for settlement despite the mountain valley's harsher winters and shorter growing seasons.

Sprouting northward from Wellsville in 1859 were Providence, Mendon, Logan, Smithfield, and Richmond. Franklin took root farther north in 1860.

The Cache Valley settlers were well aware that their presence would upset the Shoshoni. And they knew the soldiers at Camp Floyd had little interest in defending the settlements. And, as events unfolded, those soldiers would be gone in a matter of months anyway.

So, for protection from and quick response to Indian threats, each community organized a mounted militia unit—"Minute

Men." Since violence against settlers was rare, the militias may have had a deterrent effect on that score.

But stealing was another matter. The most frequent duty of the Minute Men proved to be hard riding on cold trails after stolen livestock, most often to return empty handed. In recounting one such Cache Valley pursuit, the *Deseret News* reported, "The result of the chase was that the redskins made good their escape with nearly thirty of the horses." Which, it seems, was the usual course of events. "In truth we cannot recollect a single instance within the last ten years in which a pursuit of Indians has been successful under such circumstances."[26]

In keeping with official policy, Cache Valley settlers tried to co-exist with, even support, the native Shoshoni—but they weren't always happy about it. "The people of the valley have been greatly annoyed with the Indians during the winter," a Mendon settler wrote in 1860, "and they have had to feed about two hundred of them since last fall, which has been a heavy tax," he complained, "but it had to be borne, as there was no alternative but to feed them or do worse."[27]

"The men would take their guns with them to the fields, and while one guarded the cattle, the others would plow," one early Cache Valley settler, Margaret McNiel Ballard of Logan, remembered. "My husband was a minute man and of course had to go many times without even saying goodbye, to look for the stolen cattle," she said of the summer of 1861. "We would always have a good supply of bread on hand so that we could feed the Indians and they would be more friendly toward us."[28]

But it is clear that the success of attempts to pacify the Shoshoni with foodstuffs was limited. A September, 1862, newspaper account said Indians in Cache Valley were "saucy and belligerent" toward settlers. "They are reported to be unusually fond of beef, which, if they cannot get in one way, they will take in another." Still, the report encouraged caution. "It is hoped that the people will have patience and wisdom enough to get along with the troublesome creatures, without inciting them to war and deeds of blood."[29]

On the same day, in the same column, the Salt Lake City newspaper reported that "Col. P. E. Conner, commanding the California Volunteers, arrived in the city yesterday afternoon."[30] Though neither group occupying Cache Valley could have known it at the time, one result of the soldier's arrival in Utah Territory would be a deteriorating, increasingly hostile relationship between Mormon settlers and the Shoshoni.

⁂

Salt Lake City's Mormon newspaper, the *Deseret News*, commented, with a certain skepticism, on the effectiveness, even advisability, of California Volunteer actions against the Shoshoni. In its first report on Major McGarry's November, 1862, expedition to recover stolen livestock from a Shoshoni camp near the Bear River ferry, the newspaper said, "We forbear comments till more shall have been made known concerning the expedition and its results, which we fear, if not now, will eventually prove unfavorable." In spite of its promised "forbearance" the newspaper further commented that unless the Indians had been "thoroughly whipped" and the stock recovered, "it is feared that the northern settlements will not be as safe hereafter as they were before the expedition."[31]

When it reported in a later issue McGarry's execution of four bound Shoshoni prisoners on the expedition, in which "fifty-one shots were fired before life in all of them became extinct," the newspaper further opined that the deaths "may have a salutary effect upon the natives in that region, but it is feared that it will tend to make them more hostile and vindictive."[32]

Reports of Indians stealing horses and cattle in retaliation for the executions were several during the early winter months. But, "No one has been killed by them so far as known, but it is reported on good authority that they are determined, according to their code, to have 'blood for blood'."[33]

And there was bloodshed—but it wasn't settlers' blood.

Instead, "a young Indian belonging to, or living with Mr. Jacob Meeks" near Brigham City was shot in "An Outrageous Occurrence." A group of settlers searching for stolen horses hired the young Indian as a guide, but shortly after setting out, they argued about pay. The guide refused to continue and turned for home. Reese Jones, the posse's leader, "gave chase, and on coming near enough, drew a revolver and fired at the Indian three times." Two shots missed, but the third ball entered the Indian's back and did not emerge, "inflicting a serious, and believed to be, a mortal wound."[34]

The newspaper informed readers on January 28, 1863, of the Army's "Expedition for the Arrest of Indian Chiefs." A band of opportunistic Shoshoni murdered a traveling miner in Cache Valley, providing Colonel Connor an excuse to once again invade the northern valleys in pursuit of Indians. The commander was "well supplied with guides, infantry, cavalry, howitzers, and shell to meet mountain or scientific warfare." Connor's plan for the Shoshoni, the newspaper said, was to "wipe them out" if the chiefs did not surrender.[35] The colonel, however, had already told Marshal Isaac Gibbs, who had responsibility for making the arrests, that there was no need for surrender, as he did not intend to take any prisoners.

⁂

Shoshoni history says the Indians, fearful and nervous owing to the difficulties with settlers and the attack on the miners, knew of the approaching army. One of their old men, Tindup, dreamed his people would be attacked. The vision prompted many to leave the winter camp on the Bear River at Beaver Creek near Franklin.

Also, "a white friend of the Shoshone—the owner of the grocery store in Franklin—came to the camp and told them that the settlers of Cache Valley had sent an appeal to Colonel Connor in Salt Lake City to come and settle the Indian problem." The Indians believed the settlers wanted to "completely get rid of the Northwestern Band of Shoshone."[36]

This anxiety may have been reinforced by the reported visit of Shoshoni leader Sanpitch to Brigham Young in Salt Lake City as all this unfolded. According to John A. Anderson, a chaplain in Connor's army who was also a correspondent for a number of California newspapers including the *Sacramento Daily Union*, the Mormon president told the Shoshoni chief that the Cache Valley Saints had endured enough from the Indians, and just might be inclined to "pitch in" on the side of the troops.[37]

But no matter how much or little the Shoshoni knew of the army's plans and the possibility of Mormon cooperation, it is fairly certain that three members of Bear Hunter's band—some accounts say Bear Hunter himself—while procuring wheat from the Saints' stores, saw the infantry arrive in Franklin late in the afternoon of January 28.

Franklin resident William Hull said he was sent to the granary to help sack nine bushels of wheat and load it on the three Indian pack horses. "We had two of the three horses loaded. . .when I looked up and saw the soldiers approaching from the south," Hull said. "I said to the Indian boys 'Here come the "Toquashes" (Indian name for soldiers) maybe you will all be killed.' They answered, 'maybe Toquashes be killed too'." The Indians, three bushels shy of their allotment, "quickly jumped on their horses and led the three horses away, disappearing towards the north."[38]

Whatever prevailing Mormon attitudes about the Shoshoni may have been at the time, at least one leader voiced doubt that the pending fight would serve any purpose.

"It is said that Col. Connor is determined to exterminate the Indians. . . .Small detachments have been leaving for the North for several days," George A. Smith, counselor to Brigham Young, said. "If the present expedition copies the doings of the others

Respected frontiersman and notorious gunfighter Orrin Porter Rockwell served as civilian guide for the cavalry on their journey to the Bear River Massacre. He proved instrumental in recruiting local Mormon settlers to locate the Shoshoni village before the fight and in arranging teams and sleighs to transport wounded soldiers out of Cache Valley afterward.

that preceded it, it will result in catching some friendly Indians, murdering them, and letting the guilty scamps remain undisturbed in their mountain haunts."[39]

⸎▤▧▤⸎▤▧▤⸎

Connor was equally skeptical, if not more so, about Mormon innocence concerning Shoshoni misbehavior. His belief that the Saints routinely incited the Indians found its way into many

79

official reports. So it is no surprise that he wrote after the fact that Mormons were no help in the Bear River mission; even a hindrance to the army's pursuit of its duties. "I should mention that in my march from this post [Camp Douglas] no assistance was rendered by the Mormons who seemed indisposed to divulge any information regarding the Indians."[40]

A deeper truth was that "The colonel understood only too well that no expedition of the size he contemplated could succeed without superior scouting reports and excellent piloting," according to one historian. "Clearly, Connor would need help from the Mormons. . . . All Connor's inquiries brought him the same answer—Rockwell."[41]

Orrin Porter Rockwell was among the most famous frontiersmen of his day, known from Illinois to the California gold fields. He was indisputably a cold-eyed crack shot, accomplished tracker of man and animal, horseman extraordinaire, and experienced scout. He was reputedly a cold-blooded assassin, robber, rustler, captain of the evildoing Danites, and mercenary murderer.

Thus, Connor, distrustful of all Mormons, was forced by circumstance to trust the most notorious Mormon of them all.

Other, reluctant, Saints, familiar with the local lay of the land, were employed at Franklin to show the soldiers the way to the Indian camp in the dark. So when dawn found Colonel Connor and his California Volunteers on the bluff overlooking the Shoshoni winter camp on the *Boa Ogoi* at *Moson Kahni* on January 29, 1863, it was Mormons who guided them there.

Chapter Three Notes

1. Unruh, John D., Jr. *The Plains Across: The Overland Emigrants and the Trans-Mississippi West, 1840-60.* Urbana: University of Illinois Press. Paperback edition, 1982, pp. 118-121

2. "Journal History of the Church," August 15, 1846, Archives Division, Historical Department, Church of Jesus Christ of Latter-day Saints, Salt Lake City. (Cited in Christy, Howard A. "Open Hand and Mailed Fist: Mormon-Indian Relations in Utah, 1847-52." *Utah Historical Quarterly*, Summer 1978. Volume 46, Number 3, p. 218)

3. "Journal History of the Church," August 1, 1847, Archives Division, Historical Department, Church of Jesus Christ of Latter-day Saints, Salt Lake City. (Cited in Christy, Howard A. "Open Hand and Mailed Fist: Mormon-Indian Relations in Utah, 1847-52." *Utah Historical Quarterly*, Summer 1978. Volume 46, Number 3, p. 219)

4. Smith, Joseph. *The Doctrine and Covenants of the Church of Jesus Christ of Latter-day Saints.* Salt Lake City: The Church of Jesus Christ of Latter-day Saints, 1989, p. 56

5. Smith, Joseph. *The Doctrine and Covenants of the Church of Jesus Christ of Latter-day Saints.* Salt Lake City: The Church of Jesus Christ of Latter-day Saints, 1989, p. 90

6. Pratt, Parley P. *Proclamation of the Twelve Apostles of the Church of Jesus Christ of Latter-day Saints*, dated 6 April 1845. (Cited in Arrington, Leonard J. and Bitton, Davis. *The Mormon Experience*, Second Edition. Urbana: University of Illinois Press, 1992, pp. 146-147)

7. Parry, Mae. "The Northwestern Shoshone," in *A History of Utah's American Indians*. Edited by Cuch, Forrest S. Salt Lake City: Utah State Division of Indian Affairs / Utah State Division of History, 2000, p. 25

8. Unruh, John D., Jr. *The Plains Across: The Overland Emigrants and the Trans-Mississippi West, 1840-60.* Urbana: University of Illinois Press. Paperback edition, 1982, p. 144

9. Ivan Wongan interview, "Northwestern Band of the Shoshone Nation" (video program) Norman: University of Oklahoma American Indian Institute in conjunction with Northwestern Band of the Shoshone Nation, Lewis-Clark State College Educational Technology Department, State of Idaho Department of Health and Welfare. 1992

10. Madsen, Brigham D. *The Shoshoni Frontier and the Bear River Massacre.* Salt Lake City: University of Utah Press, 1985, pp. 36-38 (Quotation from Utah State Militia Correspondence, 1849-1863, Eldredge to Ferguson, Adj. Gen., Sept. 20, 1850)

11. Young, Brigham. Manuscript History, 1850: 108, LDS Archives. (Cited in Christy, Howard A. "Open Hand and Mailed Fist: Mormon-Indian Relations in Utah, 1847-52." *Utah Historical Quarterly*, Summer 1978. Volume 46, Number 3, pp. 228-229)

12. Young, Brigham. Manuscript History, 1850: 121, LDS Archives. (Cited in Christy, Howard A. "Open Hand and Mailed Fist: Mormon-Indian Relations in Utah, 1847-52." *Utah Historical Quarterly*, Summer 1978. Volume 46, Number 3, pp. 229)

13. Roberts, Brigham H. *A Comprehensive History of the Church of Jesus Christ of Latter-day Saints.* Salt Lake City: Deseret News Press, 1930. Volume 4, p. 51

14. Young, Brigham. Sermon, 28 July, 1866, in *Journal of Discourses* 11:263. (Cited in Arrington, Leonard J. and Bitton, Davis. *The Mormon Experience*, Second Edition. Urbana: University of Illinois Press, 1992, pp. 148)

15. Parry, Mae. "The Northwestern Shoshone," in *A History of Utah's American Indians*. Edited by Cuch, Forrest S. Salt Lake City: Utah State Division of Indian Affairs / Utah State Division of History, 2000, pp. 26-29

16. Madsen, Brigham D. *The Lemhi: Sacajawea's People.* Caldwell: Caxton Printers, Ltd., 1990, pp. 34-35

17. Legislative Assembly of the Territory of Utah, Fillmore, Utah, 18 December 1855, Territorial Papers of Utah, Special Collections, Merrill Library, Utah State University. (Cited in Peterson, F. Ross. *A History of Cache County.* Salt Lake City: Utah State Historical Society and Cache County Council, 1997, p. 26)

18. Peterson, F. Ross. *A History of Cache County.* Salt Lake City: Utah State Historical Society and Cache County Council, 1997, p. 30

19. Young, Brigham. Brigham Young Papers, Maughan to Young, June 4, 1857. (Cited in Madsen, Brigham D. *The Shoshoni Frontier and the Bear River Massacre.* Salt Lake City: University of Utah Press, 1985, p. 83)

20. Young, Brigham. Cache Valley Letters, Brigham Young to Peter Maughan, Special Collections, Merrill Library, Utah State University. (Cited in Peterson, F. Ross. *A History of Cache County.* Salt Lake City: Utah State Historical Society and Cache County Council, 1997, p. 34)

21. Huntington, Dimmick Baker. Journal, August 30, 1857 (incorrectly dated September 30), MS 1419 2, LDS Archives (Cited in Bigler, David L. *Forgotten Kingdom: The Mormon Theocracy in the American West, 1847-1896.* Logan: Utah State University Press, 1998, p. 168)

22. Young, Brigham. Indian Affairs, Indian Correspondence, Young to Washakie, Nov. 2, 1857. (Cited in Madsen, Brigham D. *The Shoshoni Frontier and the Bear River Massacre.* Salt Lake City: University of Utah Press, 1985, p. 83)

23. U.S. Congress, Senate, *Message of the President*, serial 1024, p. 15. (Cited in Madsen, Brigham D. *The Shoshoni Frontier and the Bear River Massacre.* Salt Lake City: University of Utah Press, 1985, p. 89)

24. Unruh, John D. Jr. *The Plains Across: The Overland Emigrants and the Trans-Mississippi West, 1840-1860.* Urbana: University of Illinois Press, Paperback edition, 1982, p. 151

25. Burton, Sir Richard F. *The City of the Saints.* Santa Barbara: The Narrative Press, 2003, p. 329-330

26. *Deseret News*, Salt Lake City, November 19, 1862, p. 4

27. Willie, James G. Journal, Special Collections, Merrill Library, Utah State University. (Cited in Peterson, F. Ross. *A History of Cache County.* Salt Lake City: Utah State Historical Society and Cache County Council, 1997, p. 41)

28. Ricks, Joel. "Memories of Early Days in Cache County" From experiences of Margaret McNiel Ballard, "We arrived in Logan October 27th, 1859," p. 16, The Brigham D. Madsen Papers, Ms 671, Box 73, folder 1, Manuscripts Division, J. Willard Marriott Library, University of Utah

29. *Deseret News*, Salt Lake City, September 10, 1862, p. 5

30. *Deseret News*, Salt Lake City, September 10, 1862, p. 5

31. *Deseret News*, Salt Lake City, December 10, 1862, p. 4

32. *Deseret News*, Salt Lake City, December 17, 1862, p. 5

33. *Deseret News*, Salt Lake City, December 31, 1862, p. 4

34. *Deseret News*, Salt Lake City, December 31, 1862, p. 4

35. *Deseret News*, Salt Lake City, January 28, 1863, p. 4

36. Parry, Mae. "The Northwestern Shoshone," in *A History of Utah's American Indians.* Edited by Cuch, Forrest S. Salt Lake City: Utah State Division of Indian Affairs / Utah State Division of History, 2000, p. 34

37. Madsen, Brigham D. *The Shoshoni Frontier and the Bear River Massacre.* Salt Lake City: University of Utah Press, 1985, p. 179

38. Hull, William. "Identifying the Indians of Cache Valley, Utah and Franklin County, Idaho," *Franklin County Citizen*, January 25, 1928. (Cited in Madsen, Brigham D. *The Shoshoni Frontier and the Bear River Massacre.* Salt Lake City: University of Utah Press, 1985, p. 182)

39. "Journal History of the Church," January 26, 1863, George A. Smith , History of Brigham Young. The Brigham D. Madsen Papers, Ms 671, Box 74, Folder 10, Manuscripts Division, J. Willard Marriott Library, University of Utah

40. *The War of the Rebellion*, Sec. 1, Vol. 50, Part I, 186-187 (Cited in "The Battle of Bear River: A paper presented to the Fort Douglas Museum of Military History," by Captain Melvin J. Littig, USA, 1977)

41. Schindler, Harold. *Orrin Porter Rockwell: Man of God, Son of Thunder.* Salt Lake City: University of Utah Press, 1993, p. 326

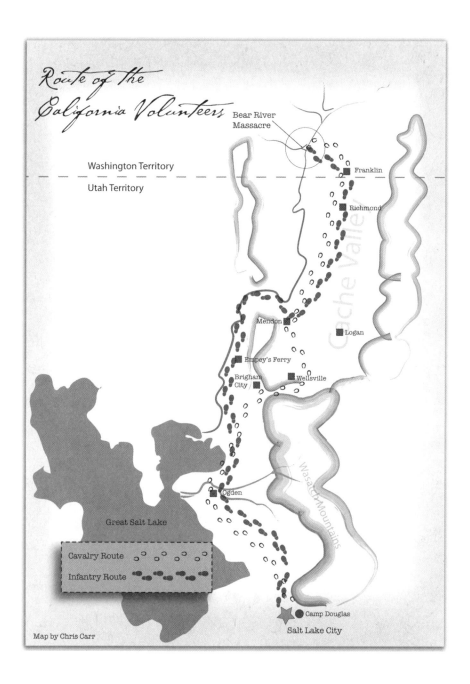

Route of the California Volunteers

Bear River Massacre

Washington Territory

Utah Territory

Franklin

Richmond

Cache Valley

Mendon

Logan

Empey's Ferry

Brigham City

Wellsville

Ogden

Wasatch Mountains

Great Salt Lake

Cavalry Route

Infantry Route

Camp Douglas

Salt Lake City

Map by Chris Carr

Chapter Four
ROUND TRIP TO A MASSACRE

Continuing with unflinching courage for over four hours you completely cut him to pieces, captured his property and arms, destroyed his stronghold, and burned his lodges.— Colonel Patrick Edward Connor

Men, who took part in that battle, boast today of taking little infants by the heels and beating their brains out on any hard substance they could find. — Be-shup (Frank Timbimboo Warner)

I feel my skirts clear of their blood. They rejected the way of life and salvation which have been pointed out to them from time to time and thus have perished relying on their own strength and wisdom. — Peter Maughan

When a cold, distant sun cleared the southeastern horizon at about a quarter past eight o'clock on the morning of January 29, 1863, the fight was well underway. By the time the sun reached its high point, low in the southern sky at noon, the killing was two hours gone.

It had taken only about four hours for Colonel Connor's California Volunteers to turn a winter camp of some seventy lodges housing 350 or more of Bear Hunter's people into a patchwork of stains in the snow.

Tipis, clothing, household goods burned down to blotches of black ash. Broad strokes of beige, yellow, and ochre brushed by castoff seeds, grains, and meal. Muddy smears, from dirty brown to clay gray.

And, everywhere on the field, the blood of the better part of the Northwestern Band of the Shoshoni spattered, speckled, and splashed in clotted scarlet. At least 250 dead Shoshoni were strewn the length of Beaver Creek ravine and on the surrounding plain. Dozens more floated lifelessly away in the icy waters of the Bear River.

On the opposite riverbank, the corpses of fourteen soldiers stiffened in the sub-freezing chill. Others, yet alive, lay suffering from frozen feet and frostbitten fingers. The army surgeon, assisted by healthy troopers, rendered aid as possible to forty-nine wounded comrades.

The first and worst of the West's Indian massacres was at an end. And in its arrangements, its innovations, its execution, it set a pattern for other armies, other engagements in years to come in the American West.

⁂

Were Westerners of the day as concerned with the niceties of law and order as they would become later, it is altogether possible the Bear River Massacre would never have happened.

In the first place, even given the confusion over the border between Utah Territory and Washington Territory, some suspected, some were sure, that the Shoshoni camp on the *Boa Ogoi* was beyond the legal jurisdiction of the Territory of Utah and the arrest warrants that justified the expedition.

But Connor felt justified in mounting the expedition no matter where he found the Indians, as he was convinced, right or wrong, that those particular Shoshoni in that particular camp "had been murdering emigrants on the Overland Mail Route for the past fifteen years."[1] Protection of the mails and the trails was, of course, the very reason for the presence of the California

Volunteers in Utah, so the commanding officer believed pursuing the perpetrators wherever the trail led was well within his rights.

Second, the Colonel also believed the Shoshoni encampment included those responsible for the murder of "several miners during the winter, passing to and from the settlements in this valley to the Beaver Head mines" of Montana.[2] Strict compliance with the law would require apprehending and bringing to trial the individuals believed responsible for the killings. The arrest warrants accompanying the mission named several chiefs, none of whom were known to be involved—or even suspected—in the murders.

Finally, and most important, Connor, by his own admission, cared little about the warrants and did not intend to make any arrests or return any prisoners for the law.

All the legalities—or lack thereof—notwithstanding, the Colonel chose a course of action then unique in American military history in many of its details, and certainly in its totality.

Never before had the military in the West launched an expedition of this scale against Indians. Most encounters to date had been skirmishes much smaller in scope. Connor sent some seventy infantrymen marching north out of Camp Douglas as a decoy force, accompanied by fifteen supply wagons. The departure of the soldiers was no secret, and in fact was widely publicized, including the false notion that the troopers were off to escort a wagon train of grain out of Cache Valley.

The main force, 220 cavalry troopers and their officers, rode out three days later, this time in secret and in the dead of night—a total force of some 300 fighting men.

The men were well armed. The supply wagons with the advance contingent of infantry carried two howitzers and 100 shells for them, and sizeable amounts of other ammunition. Each cavalry trooper carried a carbine with forty rounds of ammunition and a sidearm with thirty rounds—more than enough ammunition to kill every Indian thought to be encamped in Cache Valley several times over.

The men were well supplied. The wagons carried sufficient food for an expedition lasting twenty days. The cavalry troopers were instructed to load haversacks with three days of cooked rations, allowing for cold camps and minimal delay during the covert march.

And never before had an army in the West tested the weather to the extent Connor did. "I determined," to go ahead, the commander said, "although the season was unfavorable to an expedition in consequence of the cold weather and deep snow."[3]

All that, in theory at least, to effect the arrest of a few killers.

⁂

The Shoshoni, meanwhile, were settling in for the remainder of winter after encouraging its end with the annual Warm Dance celebration. Thousands of Shoshoni had been on hand for the festivities, including some of Washakie's people from the east. Also present was the independent-minded Pocatello and his followers, who, while numbered among the Northwestern Shoshoni, spent most of their time away from the other bands. According to tribal history, the hotheaded young warriors said to have killed the miners on the trail were members of Pocatello's band.

Foot races, horse races, hockey, dancing, and just general all-around fun occupied the villagers in the weeks leading up to January 29. But many were nervous, given the murdered miner and other difficulties with white settlers. The dream of tribal elder Tin Dup, in which he saw soldiers slaughtering The People, prompted the old man's exhortations to abandon the village, which contributed to the tension. Some took the advice, including Pocatello, who gathered most of his people and left the camp on the *Boa Ogoi* on January 28.

Tribal history also tells of a visit to the campsite by a friendly settler about the same time, who informed Indian leaders that the

Cache Valley Mormons intended to have them all killed and told them the Army was already on the way to do the job.

So, it seems, although the Shoshoni knew Connor was coming they did not believe "that the Colonel would fire first and not ask any questions."[4] According to one account, Shoshoni leaders said of the approaching troops that white men "liked to parade to show off their prowess and bravery," and "they would only parade around and go home."[5]

According to a California newspaper correspondent, the Shoshoni were well armed, "bountifully supplied with ammunition and firearms, having among them some of the finest rifles that any man would wish to lay to his face."[6] The Shoshoni say their fighters had only "bows and arrows, tomahawks, and a few rifles."[7] At least one soldier suffered multiple arrow wounds,[8] lending credence to the claim that not all the Shoshoni fighters had guns. Lack of ammunition for the guns they did have proved a problem; one account reports Indian attempts to melt lead and mold bullets as the fight raged around them.[9]

The Shoshoni were well provisioned. Military reports filed after the fact say there were enough foodstuffs in the camp "to serve the whole band for a number of months."[10] The army fed more than a thousand bushels of wheat seized at the camp to their horses. Also found were large quantities of "flour, potatoes, beef, and any amount of live chickens stolen from the settlements," along with "Indian provision—seeds, nuts, etc." Most all of it was burned or spoiled by the soldiers, "leaving enough, however, for the squaws and papooses."[11]

The Shoshoni were well mounted. A large horse herd grazed the river bottoms south of the campsite, and some 200 mounts were said to be in the village proper. Connor's troops rounded up 175 horses in the aftermath. "Out of this number," according to newspaper reports, infantry troopers selected mounts for the ride back to Camp Douglas and "earned for themselves the cognomen of the 'light cavalry'."[12]

The Shoshoni were well positioned. Steep bluffs curtain the Bear River at the Shoshoni winter camp, as the stream meanders through a half- to one-mile-wide flood plain some 200 feet lower in elevation than the surrounding countryside. The river flows generally north to south but meanders. The bluffs to the east are steep and rugged, difficult to descend on horseback and impossible for wagons at any point near the village. A dugway road cut the bluff in a gentler descent at a ford some distance downstream.

Besides the clay cliffs, the river hindered access to the camp from the nearest Mormon settlements, which were east of the stream. Some fifty yards wide through the area and three to four feet deep, the river's flow, while not swift, was powerful enough to sweep a man off his feet. In late January of 1863, floating slush and chunks of ice evidenced the low temperature of the water as well as complicating passage of the stream.

Beyond the river, a narrow plain intervened. Half to three-quarters of a mile of open and generally level terrain—depending on the exact location of the stream, which has since shifted—exposed the approach to the village. A row of thick willows fenced the verge of Beaver Creek ravine. As it coursed upstream from its level junction with the river, the ravine's sides deepened to ten or twelve feet before carving a shallow canyon into and up through the western bluffs. Trails and steps cut and worn into the banks in various places along the ravine allowed access. The floor of the ravine may have been as wide as seventy feet in some areas, and generally thick with willows and tall grass.

From the western bluffs, hard against a headland called Cedar Point, to a point in the ravine about halfway to the river, some sixty-five to seventy-five Shoshoni lodges stretched like a tangled string of beads. Some lodges were hide-covered, others with wagon canvas (many said to be marked with the names of the former owners, emigrants from whom they were stolen[13]), and some lodges were stacked limbs, brush, grass, and reeds.

Connor reported the Shoshoni village site "one of strong natural defenses, and almost inaccessible to the troops."[14] Soldiers claimed "that with the same number of troops as Indians in such a position, they could have held at bay two thousand soldiers."[15]

With the arsenal at their disposal, one can imagine the soldiers accomplishing just such a feat. But for the Shoshoni fighters that day, the advantage proved as short-lived as their ammunition.

The cavalry march to the bluffs above the Shoshoni camp on the *Boa Ogoi* is one of America's unheralded heroic efforts. The four companies—A, H, K, and M of the Second Cavalry of the California Volunteers—could scarcely have chosen a worse night to mount up and ride out of camp.

But the choice was not theirs in any case. Connor planned the day and time for secrecy's sake, weather notwithstanding. So while the infantry march two days prior had been accompanied by heavy snow, the cavalry rode out, as scheduled, under clear, cold skies, in sub-zero temperatures, and head-on into piercing arctic winds which stirred up more than a foot of freshly fallen snow.

The officers and soldiers—from Colonel Connor to Major McGarry and on down—were ill-equipped for such extreme weather, covered only in typical cavalry garb of the times reinforced by extra blankets. Twenty-five years would pass before the army routinely issued cold-weather gear suited for the mountain blizzards of the West—long buffalo overcoats, buffalo hide overshoes, muskrat caps and such.[16]

The night took its toll. As the frigid air from the north roared along the flank of the Wasatch Range, the cavalry rode from the south into its face. Faces, feet, and fingers soon numbed. Fierce winds wedged ice and snow into the gaps between the riders' feet and their stirrups, holding them fast. Breath froze on faces, icing mustaches and beards into uncomfortable clots. Canteens froze, including those filled with whiskey.

A few troopers peeled off at towns along the way, chilled beyond ability to ride on. But most braved the cold and wind and snow and "Notwithstanding that hands became powerless to hold the reins, that ears and nose were made lifeless,"[17] rode on through the night.

"Forty miles a day on beans and hay" was the conventional wisdom concerning a cavalry march in the West. That, of course, assumes daylight and reasonable weather. Under circumstances almost too difficult to imagine, the California Volunteers covered sixty-eight miles that first night on the march to Cache Valley.

For comparison, Pony Express riders generally covered seventy-five to 125 miles a day—but with the benefits of a light load and a fresh horse every fifteen miles or so. In extreme circumstances, 100 miles a day might be possible for a lone rider on a well-conditioned horse—the rider may make it, but the horse will not likely survive.

By any measure, the cavalry ride is the stuff of legend. Hired Mormon scout Porter Rockwell, a hardened frontiersman and experienced horseman who headed up the procession, had a low opinion of the soldiers at the outset. But, "His respect for the California Volunteers increased with every agonizing mile."[18]

Morning found the cavalry in cold camp at the mouth of Sardine Canyon near the town of Box Elder, or Brigham City. Following a cold and uncomfortable day of rest, the troopers remounted for another night ride—save about seventy-five of their number, whose frostbite and chilblains and hypothermia proved so severe they were unable to continue. Most of that number of frozen soldiers were left behind in Brigham City; some had dropped out in Mormon settlements along the way there.[19]

The next leg of the journey was shorter, but no less difficult. Plowing through as much as four feet of snow in the canyons cutting through the Wasatch Mountains was necessary to reach Cache Valley, where the horse soldiers caught up with their infantry troops and supply wagons the next day near the village of Mendon at the valley's western edge.

The infantry's journey had, by design, been a more leisurely affair. But it was far from easy and by no means pleasant.

After leaving Camp Douglas thirteen snowy miles behind, they camped the first night, Thursday, January 22, near Bountiful, then called Sessions Settlement. Friday night found the force twenty-five miles farther north on the banks of Weber Creek, and the troops bivouacked the third night at Willow Creek, near Willard, following a nineteen-mile march through a heavy snowstorm.

Rather than brave the rugged trail through the mountains east from Box Elder, the infantry marched northward along the cold Montana road another sixteen miles to Empey's Bear River Ferry. From there the next morning, Monday, January 26, the marchers and wagons crossed a gentler divide eastward into Cache Valley. While the terrain here was less rugged than Sardine Canyon east of Box Elder, conditions were not. Deep snow, crusted over in many areas, covered the road and back-breaking labor was needed to break trail for many of the twenty-five miles. The detachment set up a final camp near Mendon in Cache Valley to await the January 27 arrival of the clandestine cavalry force.

A California newspaper reported the infantry had "marched through snow all day, sleeping in the same all night" and made the trip "with a rapidity, and bearing its terrible fatigues with fortitude rarely equaled and never excelled by the armies of any nation."[20]

Captain Charles H. Hempstead, remembering the difficulties of the journey in an anniversary oration a year later, said the troops "faced the severity of winter in the mountains and pressed on; the Infantry by day and the Cavalry by night, to deceive the wily foe."[21]

In official documents from the expedition, Colonel Connor could not resist a dig at the Mormons. "I should mention here that in my march from this post no assistance was rendered by the Mormons, who seemed indisposed to divulge any information regarding the Indians," he reported, "and charged enormous prices for every article furnished my command."[22]

And so the California Volunteers were positioned in Cache Valley, according to Connor's plan, to launch an attack on the Shoshoni camp on Beaver Creek.

In keeping with his ruse to mislead the Shoshoni, Connor ordered only his infantry troops to march north to Franklin—the final Mormon settlement in Cache Valley and the nearest to the Indian's winter camp. They left just before midnight, Tuesday, January 27, for the thirty-mile trip, arriving in Franklin about four o'clock the next afternoon. Among the witnesses of their arrival were two or three young Shoshoni men fetching wheat from the Mormon granary; the first sure knowledge the Indians had of the soldiers' presence.

The cavalry followed up from Mendon a few hours later, but halted their ride twenty miles later at Summit Creek, or Smithfield, at eight in the morning—twelve miles south of Franklin. There they stayed until ten o'clock that night, then rode on to Franklin, where, at half past midnight on the new morning of Thursday, January 29, the horse soldiers once again caught up with the foot soldiers.

Connor intended for the slower-moving infantry, with howitzers and ammunition in tow, to leave town at one in the morning. The Colonel and the cavalry would depart two hours later, with the intention of reuniting the forces near the battlefield while darkness prevailed, allowing time for the soldiers to surround the encampment and attack at dawn.

The plan failed when none of the settlers were inclined to guide the army to a place near the Indian village where it would be possible to ford the Bear River. The march was delayed for two hours until local scouts became available—brothers Edmund and Joseph Nelson—following a good deal of heavy-handed encouragement by their Mormon leaders.[23]

Beginning to worry that the Shoshoni would somehow learn of his intentions and skedaddle, Connor set out with the cavalry only an hour after the infantry got underway, and overtook them too soon—the village was yet four miles distant. The commander's anxiety increased upon seeing his howitzers and supply wagons wallowing and bogged in deep snow. Cache Valley settlers, experienced with winter travel cross-country and over unreliable roads, had long since learned to replace wheels with runners during the depth of winter. Connor either did not know or did not learn the lesson.

So, he sent McGarry and the cavalry onward and stayed behind to sort out the mess with the artillery and infantry. After a futile struggle and seeing no alternative, the colonel ordered the howitzers abandoned, told the foot soldiers to hurry, and rode ahead to see what his major had found upon reaching the river.

⁂

The seeming simplicity of Connor's strategy, seen through modern lenses fogged by intervening military history, belies its many innovations.

While war can never be considered only a fair-weather activity, instigating a battle in deep snow and sub-zero temperatures was unusual. Armies—United States and Indian alike—tended to hunker down for the season, much as Washington's troops went into winter quarters at Valley Forge. Cold weather may well prove a more formidable enemy than opposing armies, as Napoleon learned in Russia.

And yet Connor opted to utilize the storms and cold as an ally. Adventuring forth with a sizeable army in such unfavorable conditions, contrary to pattern and common sense, supported his deception of the Shoshoni concerning his intentions.

Military tradition, regardless of the strategies or tactics involved, also dictated that armies fight other armies. Combatants fought on battlefields, often of the defender's choosing, often on the run, but selected—as much as possible—to accommodate the fight. Troops were usually lured out of barracks or camps to fight in the open. Fortified positions were often attacked, but seldom was a battle fought within the confines of an occupied village or settlement where noncombatants might be endangered.

Likely knowing full well that the majority of the Shoshoni village's occupants would be old men, women, and children rather than fighters, Connor still planned to catch the occupants of the winter camp sleeping, attack by surprise, and kill whatever moved. The colonel's hometown newspaper reported that he "gave strict orders against killing women and children, of whom, contrary to precedent, there were a large number in the camp." Despite the orders, the same correspondent claimed "a few were slightly wounded, and I believe one killed."[24] While the actual number of noncombatants killed cannot be known with certainty, "one" grossly underestimates the carnage.

Battlefield tactics of the early Civil War were little changed from those practiced by opposing armies for many, many years. From earlier military training and service in the Mexican War, Colonel Connor was familiar with the accepted practice of deploying troops in battle lines, marching forward until near the enemy's position, firing a volley, then charging with bayonets. Flanking the enemy or maneuvering to attack from the rear were sometimes attempted by more adventurous battle strategists, but lack of effective communications, command, and control meant such endeavors usually disintegrated in chaos.[25]

For whatever reason, the Colonel planned an untraditional deployment of the California Volunteers. His scheme called for the troops to arrive at the village before daylight, encircle it, and shoot down the Shoshoni without losing a single soldier.[26] To surround the camp was the order given cavalry commander McGarry when

Author's photo
Attacking cavalry forded the river near this point to attack the Shoshoni camp.

sent ahead of the stalled infantry—but, upon reaching the field, the major realized the impossibility of that strategy given geography and the shortage troops. So when insults shouted from Shoshoni lines raised McGarry's ire and lured him to attack before Connor and the foot soldiers arrived, he formed his troops into a traditional battle line for a frontal attack.

It would prove a mistake.

A cavalcade the size of McGarry's cavalry can only be kept secret for so long. Sooner or later, 150 riders and their horses—the approximate size of the force that poured over the Bear River bluffs the morning of January 29, 1863—are bound to be noticed.

Whether a fog of horse sweat, steamy breath blown from flared nostrils, or clouds of snow churned up by 600 hooves, something created a haze that attracted the notice of Sagwitch. The early rising Shoshoni chief is said to have wandered out of his lodge in the pre-dawn darkness for a look around the neighborhood when he noticed "something up on the ridge there" that looked "like a

97

cloud." He wondered if it could be steam from horses belonging to "them soldiers they were talking about."[27]

As the haze or mist crept down the bluff while Sagwitch watched from the village some three-quarters of a mile away, he determined it must be the cavalry. And while he fully expected that he, Bear Hunter, and other chiefs would likely meet with the officers for negotiations, he took the precaution of waking the village and encouraged the fighting men to arm themselves and prepare for battle.[28]

Having made their way down the steep face of the 200-foot bluff east of the Bear River, the California Volunteers found themselves faced with the river itself. Carrying out the attack on the Shoshoni winter camp necessitated fording fifty and more yards of black water three to four feet deep, partly frozen, streaming with mushy ice and snow and hard-frozen chunks of ice. Both horses and riders paled at the task of a crossing in the cold and dark.

Trooper John S. Lee remembered the fear he felt there on the banks of "a bad looking river, half frozen over and swift. The horses did not want to go in it. Two old boys got throwed by their horses."[29] While only a few soldiers suffered a head-to-toe ice-water soaking in sub-zero temperatures owing to unfortunate horsemanship, a California newspaper correspondent reported the river's depth meant "nearly every man got his feet wet, which . . .was felt severely."[30]

Confusion apparently set in as events unfolded, as accounts about what happened next differ, even among eyewitnesses.

Perhaps the only account that cannot be questioned is that of Moroni Timbimboo, who learned about the battle from his grandfather, Sagwitch. And the only reason this account does not contradict others is its stark simplicity and lack of detail: "They [soldiers] forded the Bear River and come upon the Indians to battle with them."[31]

But the particulars of how that happened, as reported by others, vary.

Courtesy of the Church Archives, the Church of Jesus Christ of Latter-day Saints

The man in this photograph, identified by the photographer as Se-go-witz, may well be Sagwitch, a Shoshoni leader and survivor of the Bear River Massacre. Sagwitch was instrumental in holding a small band of survivors together following the massacre, seeking accommodation and acceptance with the Mormon settlers while maintaining cultural identity and integrity. Years later, following Sagwitch's lead, hundreds of Shoshoni joined the Mormon church.

Mae Parry's account, compiled from various oral histories passed down in the tribe as well as from personal research, says that while many Shoshoni men armed themselves and took up defensive positions, Sagwitch, hoping for negotiations, discouraged any "hostile action" by his people. But "The soldiers came down the bluff and charged across the river, firing their rifles as they came," she writes.[32]

Connor's report claims the Shoshoni weren't nearly so serene or self controlled. Although not on the scene when the battle was joined—he was still some miles away, encouraging the infantry with their snowbound artillery and stuck supply wagons to hurry—the version of events he recorded claims that McGarry's premature strike resulted from bait dangled by the Shoshoni. "The Indians," he said, "sallied out of their hiding places on foot and horseback, and with fiendish malignity waved the scalps of white women and challenged the troops to battle, at the same time attacking them."[33]

Eyewitnesses from among Mormon settlers in Franklin recorded their own version of events. William Hull followed the baggage wagons and arrived on the scene just at sunrise. His account has Bear Hunter tempting the troops on the bluffs above to come down and fight. The chief, "swinging his buffalo robe in the air came forward and shouted, 'Come on you California —————, we're ready for you!'"[34]

In a letter to Cache Valley Mormon leader Peter Maughan, written the day after the battle by Franklin resident and "your brother in the Gospel" Alexander Stalker, told "as far as my knowledge extends in the matter," what happened. The Shoshoni made "a demonstration" when the soldiers arrived at the riverbank, "running up and down the margin of the ravine, whooping and yelling; they also fired a gun."[35]

The newspaper correspondent from the *San Francisco Evening Bulletin* said the Shoshoni "posted some 50 mounted warriors along the plain, doubtless with the design of decoying our men into a charge."[36] *The Sacramento Daily Union's* "Occasional Correspondent" contributed a series of articles on the expedition, and his report says the "savages appeared in the bottom on horseback, shouting in derision, and beckoning them on to the fight." Another factor contributing to the cavalry's attack prior to the arrival of infantry support, according to the correspondent, was the impossibility of enduring the cold.[37]

A more inflammatory account of the fight's dawning moments appeared in Salt Lake City's *Deseret News*. The newspaper did not have a reporter on the scene, but compiled its story from information "freely furnished" by the California Volunteers. The Indians "seemed to look upon the coming struggle with particularly good humor," the story goes. It then reports a mounted chief waving a menacing spear at the soldiers, supported by a concerted effort among the Shoshoni to raise the ire of McGarry and his cavalry by calling out insults in cadence. "Fours right, fours left; come on you California sons of b———hs!

"On such a polite invitation, the word was given to 'advance.'"[38]

⁂

Recall as the fighting begins that the Shoshoni winter camp at *Boa Ogoi* occupied the floor of a shallow ravine that snaked generally southward across the river bottoms from the irregular western bluffs until it met the bending river about three-quarters of a mile later. The village occupied the upper, westernmost half of the ravine, tucked around a headland called Cedar Point, and continued upstream along Beaver Creek into the beginnings of the bluff.

Naturally defensible, the ravine's near-vertical eastern edge shielded its protectors, and thick willows lining the edge provided further cover. In order to reach the Shoshoni fortress, attacking troopers had to cross a half-mile of open bottomland that offered little in the way of cover for individual troopers and no concealment for an attacking battle line.

McGarry ordered his command forward toward the camp. Partway across the narrow plain he called a halt, dismounted all but the officers, and detailed one of every four troopers to hold the horses while the rest advanced the attack afoot.

As the attackers neared the ravine, the defending Shoshoni unleashed withering fire from concealed positions. Men went down "like the leaves of autumn."[39] As many as twenty troopers were wounded, and it's likely most of the fourteen soldiers killed in the battle fell in the opening minutes.

Connor arrived on the field soon after McGarry's foray and immediately saw the futility of a frontal assault. "[I]n consequence of being exposed on a level and open plain while the Indians were under cover, they had every advantage of us fighting with the ferocity of demons." The colonel employed the cavalry horses to ferry the infantry troops across the frigid river, and the first twenty to arrive were detailed to McGarry for a flanking move up the western bluff. As foot soldiers continued to reach the field, Connor moved them up in support of the dismounted cavalry and sent a detachment southward along the ravine to turn the Shoshoni's right flank. The tactics gave the Volunteers "the advantage of an enfilading fire," the colonel reported, and "after flanking them we had the advantage and made good use of it."[40]

"Arrows and tomahawks did little against the rifles and side arms of the soldiers," Shoshoni accounts say. "The Shoshone men, women, children, and babies were being slaughtered like rabbits, butchered by Colonel Connor and his troops."[41]

⊰▤▐▤⊱▤▐▤⊰▤▐▤⊱▤⊱

With the Shoshoni already running short of ammunition, flanked on both sides and with soldiers soon to be in their rear, the nature of the fight changed. A hard-fought battle became in turn and in its parts a rout, wanton slaughter, brutal torture, wholesale rape.

In a word, a massacre.

Sometime, some way, the California Volunteers raged out of control and the command structure either deteriorated or the commanders participated in the destruction of the Shoshoni. The behavior of the officers wants examination, but the reports are scant and contradictory.

A newspaper correspondent paints those leading the Volunteers in gallant colors. Colonel Connor remained calm throughout the fight, the news report said, and seemed not "to hear the snakish whistle of the bullets" as he directed the troops and set an "example of cool gallantry."

Cavalry Captain Price, the story said, "handled his men, and handled his pistols as effectively as any one could desire." Lieutenant Clark's guns blazed often, it was said, as if he considered "the whole operation as a sort of turkey affair."[42]

Connor honored his subordinates' battlefield behavior in official documents. "I take great pleasure in awarding to Major McGarry... Major Gallagher and Surg. R.K. Reid. . .the highest praise for their skill, gallantry, and bravery throughout the engagement," he said, "and to the company officers the highest praise is due. . .for their bravery, courage, and determination evidenced throughout the engagement."[43]

A lowly cavalry sergeant of Company K told a different story. After commanding the soldiers to attack, "no officer was heeded or needed. . . .It was a free fight every man on his own hook," he wrote in a personal account as he recuperated from frozen feet in the Camp Douglas infirmary.[44]

Whether under direct orders from superiors or on their own hook, there is little doubt from available evidence that upon gaining the advantage, the California Volunteers ripped into the Shoshoni village with purpose and determination, and kept at it for hours.

From their flanking position partway up the hill, McGarry's troopers hammered fire into the village below. Soon, the ferocity of the attack intensified as soldiers crossed the gully eroded into the bluff by Beaver Creek and maneuvered up the opposite slope, then followed a stream of lead down the ravine toward the village. At the same time, soldiers closed off the downstream end and poured fire into the opposite end of the camp, even as another detachment crossed the lower ravine and took up positions behind the village.

Although not executed as originally intended, Connor's plan was, by now, essentially accomplished: the Shoshoni were surrounded.

Loading and firing the muzzle loading rifles of the era was nearly impossible, with fingers stiff and unfeeling in the frigid air. According to reports by a "special correspondent" to the *Sacramento Daily Union* newspaper, some soldiers' fingers were so cold they "could not tell they had a cartridge in their hands unless they looked for it there."[45]

Despite the difficulty, the Volunteers laid down enough fire that the Shoshoni said dry leaves were "flying through the air along with bullets"[46] and "the willows began to fall as if they were being mowed by a scythe."[47]

It's probable frozen fingers made capping nipples on revolvers as difficult as loading a rifle. But that difficulty, too, was overcome as sidearms became the preferred weapon when the soldiers infiltrated the village and the fight turned to close quarters. Finding themselves bottled up, the Shoshoni fought with all they had, which by now wasn't much—with scarce ammunition used up, it was mostly bows and arrows, tomahawks and knives against rifles and revolvers, bayonets and swords.

Mormon witnesses reported the Shoshoni were driven down the ravine toward soldiers waiting there who "found their revolvers of incalculable value, the Indians crowding upon them were shot at arm's length in the face."[48]

It seems certain in hindsight that after two or more hours of bloody battle, the Shoshoni were defeated. "But the victory was not yet won," Sergeant Beach said. The "infuriated Volunteers" waded into the fight and "the work of death commenced in real earnest." Indian cries for quarters were heard over the din of gunfire, "but their was no quarters that day."[49] A California newspaper correspondent offered the differing view that the Shoshoni never asked for quarters, instead fought "wound for wound" until the last.[50]

Escape offered the best hope of Shoshoni survival, and the Bear River the best avenue for escape. Some made it, more died trying.

Sagwitch was shot in the hand in the crossing, but managed to ford the *Boa Ogoi* horseback while towing another man who clung to his mount's tail. Ray Diamond swam the stream and hid out in the hills. An old man effectively shielded himself from bullets by swimming the river under a heavy buffalo robe. Anzee-chee, wounded twice, swam under an overhang on the bank and survived, head barely above water in the frigid shelter. Her baby drowned, the lifeless body left to drift downstream amidst ice and swirling blood.[51]

Connor's report to his superiors said very few Shoshoni even attempted escape, but that most who made it out of the ravine "were afterward shot in attempting to swim the river" or in the "dense willow thicket which lined the river banks."[52] A narrow willow-covered island a short way downstream was a hopeful refuge for some fleeing Shoshoni but, according to Sergeant Beach, circumstances belied its promise—they found "an unwelcome reception by a few of the boys who were waiting the approach of straglers."[53]

Just how many dead Shoshoni were carried away in the river's current cannot be known. Franklin settlers who visited the massacre field the next day "understood" that most of the dead went into the river, either killed there trying to escape, or the bodies dragged from where they fell in the ravine and thrown into the stream.[54]

Most of those who stayed in the camp fared no better. For the soldiers, "it was more like a frollick than a fight" according to Sergeant Beach.[55] But reports from the military offer few particulars.

Shoshoni accounts passed down through the generations are chilling in their detail. Take the death of Bear Hunter. Whipped, kicked, tortured, and shot, the chief reportedly sat silent until a bayonet, heated in the fires of burning lodges, was thrust through his head "ear to ear." Soquitch survived the battle, escaping on a fleet horse, but his girlfriend, riding double behind him, fell dead from the mount when shot in the back. Long after the fight ended, the Shoshoni say soldiers remained on the field murdering those found alive by splitting open heads with an axe.[56]

Much of what is known of the massacre comes from accounts of Mormon settlers from Franklin. Porter Rockwell, at Connor's request, arranged for a number of villagers to bring sleighs to the river the morning after the fight to transport dead and wounded soldiers and battlefield spoils. While his sledge was being loaded, teamster William Nelson rode to the edge of the campground where lodges still smoldered, counted seventy-six bodies in the creek bottom, and assumed—from what soldiers told him—that many more lay elsewhere in the bushes and along the river.[57]

The same day, the Mormon bishop in Franklin detailed three other men to search out Indian survivors. One of them, William Hull, said there were "dead bodies everywhere. I counted eight deep in one place, and in several places they were three to five deep."[58] Alexander Stalker, in a letter to Peter Maughan, verified one Shoshoni claim: "Those of them that were not killed outright I have been told by some of the soldiers, were killed by being hit in the head with an axe."[59]

106

Infanticide, committed in the guise of mercy killing, was reported by James Martineau. He also learned of instances of rape and the murder of Shoshoni women who would not submit—some of whom were "ravished in the agony of death." Samuel Roskelley was also told by a Shoshoni named Matigund of rapes committed by solders. Israel Clark passed along reports to Mormon leaders that soldiers brutally raped women "in the act of dying from their wounds" and said the information had been "substantiated by others that were present at the time."[60]

Memories of survival are far fewer. One account comes from Be-shup, later adopted—or purchased—by a Mormon family and raised as Frank Timbimboo Warner. "Just think, at the tender age of two years receiving seven wounds which I carry today as a souvenir of that merciless battle," he wrote, "when women and sucking babes met their deaths at the hand of civilization."[61] The boy escaped death by hiding in a small grass tipi until the soldiers left, then wandered dazed and traumatized through the destroyed village until rescued by relatives.[62]

Yeager, an older brother of Be-shup, hid in a brush shelter with his grandmother and several other Shoshoni. Fearing the marauding soldiers would set the place ablaze, the old woman took the boy out among the bodies with a plan to lie on the frozen ground and feign death. Despite his grandmother's repeated instructions to keep his eyes closed and stay still, the cold and curiosity were too much for the twelve-year-old boy. When the soldiers came around prodding bodies with bayonets in order to extinguish any sign of lingering life, Yeager opened his eyes for a look only to see a trooper looking back. The boy closed his eyes for a time, then opened them and found himself staring down the barrel of the same trooper's gun. The soldier lowered the weapon and Yeager again closed his eyes. The ritual was repeated a third time, after which the soldier walked away.[63]

As night finally fell on the darkest day the Northwestern Shoshoni had ever known, the survivors at the campsite and those who had escaped gathered at open fires, and huddled cold and hungry through the night. Seeing no alternative, at first light they set out to find shelter among other bands; some to seek out Pocatello and his people to the west in Malad Valley, others toward Shoshoni winter camps to the southwest at Promontory. A few had been taken to Franklin for care by settlers.

The rest of the band, the dead, were left on the battlefield.

The California Volunteers saw to it that little else was left on the battlefield. Lodgepoles, dragged to the makeshift soldier camp across the Bear River, fed fires that provided scarce warmth through the long winter night. Everything else the Shoshoni had assembled in the way of shelter was torched, the fires heaped with clothing, camp equipment, unwanted foodstuffs, and whatever else the soldiers did not care to appropriate for their own use. What would not burn was scattered and trampled in the snow and mud.

Connor said, "I captured 175 horses, some arms, destroyed seventy lodges, a large quantity of wheat and other provisions . . .left a small quantity of wheat for the sustenance of 160 captive squaws and children, whom I left on the field."[64] Other "trophies" of war taken by individual soldiers included "buffalo robes, gewgaws, beads, pipes, tomahawks, knives, arrows, and all such things." Large amounts of beef, flour, potatoes, chickens, seeds, nuts, berries were "destroyed by the troops, leaving enough, however, for the squaws and papooses."[65]

Also seized were "numerous evidences of emigrant plunder." Found in the camp were "modern cooking utensils, looking glasses, combs, brushes," and firearms. "Lying around and patching up the wickiups" were wagon covers, some said to be marked with the names of their former owners.[66]

Having destroyed what they did not want or could not use and carting off the rest, the army left the battlefield for Camp Douglas. Like the Shoshoni, they left the bodies of dead Indians littering the massacre field when they left.

Just how many bodies there were to leave is difficult to pin down. Contemporary reports vary; some within understandable limits, others wildly. A painstaking examination of all available accounts by meticulous historian Brigham D. Madsen resulted in a best estimate of at least 250 Shoshoni killed:

Connor's official report said 224 bodies were left on the field.

Another officer noted the same number but added fifty more dead who went down the river.

Indian agent James Doty said the Shoshoni told him 255 were killed.

A Mormon settler was told by a Shoshoni that about ninety of his people died.

Another Shoshoni report claimed more than 200 dead; yet another said "There ain't no 200 Indians killed," but far fewer than that.

The body count in contemporary newspaper reports varied from 225 to 300; one correspondent estimated 225 to 267 killed.

Mormons recorded in various places 175 killed, about 200 killed, 210 killed, 225 killed, exactly 368 Indians killed.

The official Mormon version recorded "some 250 men, women and children."[67]

Sergeant Beach of the Volunteers said the Indians lost "two hundred and eighty Kiled."[68]

The number of likely noncombatant Shoshoni killed is even more difficult to establish. No one mentioned the number of old men who fell. Reports of slaughtered women and children disagree. Connor's official military report mentions total casualties with no reference to noncombatants killed.

From other reports:

Three women and two children "accidentally" killed.

Ten women.

Thirty women and many children.

Ninety women and children killed.

Two hundred and sixty-five women and children.

Thirty women dead.

About ninety squaws and children killed.[69]

Equally difficult to determine is how many Shoshoni lived. Connor reported there were 300 Shoshoni fighting men in the village he attacked.[70] Based on his own estimate of seventy-five lodges along Beaver Creek and assuming an average of five to six people in each lodge, it is unlikely there were more than 400 Shoshoni in the camp. The colonel's report claims 160 survivors. With 250 killed an acceptable estimate, from a village of perhaps 400, the possibility of 160 survivors seems reasonable.

Cache Valley journalist and historian Newell Hart devoted years to studying the massacre. After ferreting out and collecting documentary evidence, personal histories, and stories from numerous sources he arrived at his own accounting of the size of the camp, the total Shoshoni killed, and the number of survivors.

Estimating seventy lodges each with six to eight occupants, he believed the size of the village was probably between 420 and 560. Around sixty Shoshoni either survived the massacre, escaped, or left the camp shortly before the soldiers arrived, leaving 360 killed. He also believed Connor's number of dead, 224, probably did not include women and children.[71]

No matter the numbers, the disheartened and demoralized Shoshoni survivors were said to have drifted to at least two places of immediate refuge: Pocatello's village in nearby Malad Valley[72] and to another Shoshoni band wintering a bit farther away at Promontory, Utah.[73] Before long, many dispersed to join other, related bands including the Fort Hall Shoshoni, Washakie's Eastern Shoshoni, Western Shoshoni bands in Nevada, and even the Ute tribe on a reservation in the Uintah Basin to the south and east.[74]

So, the refugees from the winter camp at *Boa Ogoi* never got together to count heads.

Reported among the dead were "Chiefs Bear-Hunter, Sagwitch and Lehi."[75] Despite being listed among the killed in some contemporary reports (as well as on a battlefield memorial erected nearly seven decades later) Sagwitch survived along with several members of his family—including sons Soquitch, Yeager, and Be-shup. The surviving chief and his descendants have proved instrumental ever since in the continuing survival of the Northwestern Shoshoni band.

Sagwitch's son Be-shup, Frank Timbimboo Warner, refuted a 1918 newspaper report that he "was the only survivor of that fight." He said he wished "to make it plain as to how many escaped." Two brothers and a sister-in-law lived, as well as "many" who later lived at the Washakie, Utah settlement, the Fort Hall reservation, in the Wind River country, and elsewhere. Although he never gave a number for the survivors, Be-shup wrote that "half of those present, got away" and that 156 were killed.[76] So, if the 156 killed represented half the band, then his number for survivors, also 156, appears compatible with other estimates, despite his much lower total of Shoshoni killed.

Shoshoni historian and tribal leader Mae Timbimboo Parry, granddaughter of massacre survivor Yeager, named thirteen survivors who lived at Washakie, Utah "a living historical source of this tragic event": Sagwitch, Soquitch, Yeager, Ray Diamond, Peter Ottogary, Hyrum Wo-go-saw, Be-shup, Tin-dup (and family), Bia-Wu-Utsee (widow of Bear Hunter), Towenge (married after the massacre to Soquitch), Anzee-chee, Techa-mo-da-key, and Mo-jo-guitch.[77]

And so, despite the death blow dealt the band at the massacre at *Boa Ogoi*, the Northwestern Shoshoni survived.

<hr/>

The casualties suffered by the California Volunteers are well documented and known with exactness. Fourteen died on the field, two died from wounds on the trip home, six others succumbed to wounds after reaching Camp Douglas for a total of twenty-two deaths.

Forty-nine soldiers suffered wounds of various severity. Seventy-nine troopers were incapacitated to some degree from the effects of intense cold.

In total, the Bear River expedition claimed 142 casualties among the soldiers.

Following the fight, dead and living alike were carried back across the Bear River in the waning light for a long, cold night, many in the open air with little or no protection. Some warmth resulted from burning Shoshoni lodge poles plundered from the camp. Other than that, only green willows, reluctant to burn and emitting little heat, were available for firewood.

While the soldiers shivered, civilian scout Porter Rockwell rustled up a fleet of eighteen sleds, with teams and teamsters, from among his Mormon brethren in Franklin. Connor, "in his big heart," decreed that the dead soldiers would be transported back to Camp Douglas for burial.[78] So, conveyance was required for the dead, the wounded, and those whose frozen feet hindered their ability to walk, or ride cavalry mounts or captured Shoshoni horses.

The day after the fight, the Volunteers were transported to Franklin and when they arrived that evening, found beds of straw and warm fires at the meeting house. Some were lodged in homes. All in all, the community claimed "a united effort was made to administer comfort to the weary, wounded fighters."[79]

Similar accommodations were made available the next night in Logan, supplemented with advantages the larger community could offer. In addition to meals and beds, the citizens hosted parties for the Volunteers. California newspapers reported the soldiers were treated well by settlers in communities all along the road home. The *Deseret News* reported likewise, declaring happiness that the Mormon settlers "contributed in every way they could to their comfort."[80]

Despite the best efforts of the settlers to see the soldiers safely home to Camp Douglas, the trip was not an easy one. After the restful night in Logan and a hot breakfast, a painful parade of mounted soldiers, wounded and incapacitated troopers in sleighs driven by hired Mormons, and dead Volunteers in army baggage wagons, headed south through the valley and up the canyon. There, the caravan cut a slow, cold road through deep snow every step of the way. High winds drifted the track full almost as fast as it was made, forcing every hoof and every foot to flounder through the drifts as if there were no trail at all.

So the army turned back to enjoy another night of Mormon hospitality, this time courtesy of the citizens of Wellsville. Come morning, Mormon bishop Peter Maughan pressed every available man into service to break trail for the soldiers, and Sardine Canyon was conquered. The night of February 2 passed in camp near Brigham City, where the cavalry had laid over nine days earlier following their secretive night ride from Salt Lake City.

Then, on to Ogden, where additional medical aid dispatched from Camp Douglas was available. Mormon Apostles John Taylor and George A. Smith were in town when the soldiers arrived, "and were round among them, kindly encouraging everybody."[81]

Military wagons met the homebound expedition the next day at Farmington to hurry the soldiers southward, with the first arrivals reaching Salt Lake City about five o'clock on February 4.[82]

Unbeknownst to anyone at the time, the California Volunteers had completed a round trip to the deadliest Indian massacre in Western history. And nothing in the further history of Indian wars in the West would change that fact.

Chapter Four Notes

1. Official Report of P. Edw. Connor, February 6, 1863. (Cited in Hart, Newell. *The Bear River Massacre*, Preston: Cache Valley Newsletter Publishing Company, Second Printing 1983, p. 81)
2. Official Report of P. Edw. Connor, February 6, 1863. (Cited in Hart, Newell. *The Bear River Massacre*, Preston: Cache Valley Newsletter Publishing Company, Second Printing 1983, p. 81)
3. Official Report of P. Edw. Connor, February 6, 1863. (Cited in Hart, Newell. *The Bear River Massacre*, Preston: Cache Valley Newsletter Publishing Company, Second Printing 1983, p. 81)
4. Parry, Mae. "Massacre at Boa Ogoi." Madsen, Brigham D. *The Shoshoni Frontier and Bear River Massacre*, Salt Lake City: University of Utah Press, Appendix B, p.233
5. Washines, Lorena. "Oral History Interview with Lee Neaman" Logan: Utah State University, 1979. Special Collections, Utah State University, Merrill-Cazier Library, PAM C 109
6. *Sacramento Daily Union*, February 17, 1863 (Cited in McPherson, Robert S. *Staff Ride Handbook for the Battle of Bear River—29 January 1863*, Riverton: Utah National Guard, 2000, p. 51)
7. Parry, Mae. "Massacre at Boa Ogoi." Madsen, Brigham D. *The Shoshoni Frontier and Bear River Massacre*, Salt Lake City: University of Utah Press, Appendix B, p.233
8. Record located on the Internet, http://www.militarymuseum.org/2dCavVC.html. *California State Military Department, "The California Military Museum."* Information "Extracted from *Records of California Men in the War of the Rebellion, 1861 To 1867.*"
9. Lorenzo H. Handy Interview, in Madsen, Brigham D. *The Shoshoni Frontier and Bear River Massacre*, Salt Lake City: University of Utah Press, 1985, p.181)
10. *Record of California Men in the War of the Rebellion*, cited in Hance, Irma Watson and Warr, Irene. *Johnston, Connor, and the Mormons: An Outline of Military History in Northern Utah*, Salt Lake City: privately published, 1962, p. 74
11. *Sacramento Daily Union*, February 17, 1863 (Cited in Hart, Newell. *The Bear River Massacre*, Preston: Cache Valley Newsletter Publishing Company, Second Printing 1983, pp. 106)
12. *Sacramento Daily Union*, February 17, 1863 (Cited in Hart, Newell. *The Bear River Massacre*, Preston: Cache Valley Newsletter Publishing Company, Second Printing 1983, pp. 106-107)
13. *Sacramento Daily Union*, February 17, 1863 (Cited in Hart, Newell. *The Bear River Massacre*, Preston: Cache Valley Newsletter Publishing Company, Second Printing 1983, pp. 106)
14. Official Report of P. Edw. Connor, February 6, 1863. (Cited in Hart, Newell. *The Bear River Massacre*, Preston: Cache Valley Newsletter Publishing Company, Second Printing 1983, p. 82)
15. *Alta California*, February 7, 1863. (Cited in Hart, Newell. *The Bear River Massacre*, Preston: Cache Valley Newsletter Publishing Company, Second Printing 1983, p. 111)
16. Nevin, David. *The Old West: The Soldiers*, New York: Time-Life Books, 1973, p. 107
17. *San Francisco Daily Bulletin*, February 20, 1863. (Cited in Hart, Newell. *The Bear River Massacre*, Preston: Cache Valley Newsletter Publishing Company, Second Printing 1983, p. 92)
18. Schindler, Harold. *Orrin Porter Rockwell: Man of God, Son of Thunder*, Salt Lake City: University of Utah Press, Second Edition, 1983, p. 327
19. National Archives, "California Regt'l Order Book. 2nd Cavalry. Adjutant General's Office," Special Orders No. 11. (Cited in Madsen, Brigham D. *The Shoshoni Frontier and the Bear River Massacre*, Salt Lake City: University of Utah Press, 1985, p. 182)
20. *San Francisco Daily Bulletin*, February 20, 1863. (Cited in Hart, Newell. *The Bear River Massacre*, Preston: Cache Valley Newsletter Publishing Company, Second Printing 1983, p. 92)
21. *Union Vedette*, January 30, 1864, p. 1
22. P. Edw. Connor, Official Report, February 6, 1863. (Cited in Hart, Newell. *The Bear River Massacre*, Preston: Cache Valley Newsletter Publishing Company, Second Printing 1983, p. 82)
23. Hart, Newell. *The Bear River Massacre*, Preston: Cache Valley Newsletter Publishing Company, Second Printing 1983, p. 80

24. *Stockton Daily Independent*, February 17, 1863 (Cited in Hart, Newell. *The Bear River Massacre*, Preston: Cache Valley Newsletter Publishing Company, Second Printing 1983, p. 116)

25. McPherson. Robert S. *Staff Ride Handbook for the Battle of Bear River—29 January 1863*, Riverton: Utah National Guard, pp. 14-16

26. Hart, Newell. *The Bear River Massacre*, Preston: Cache Valley Newsletter Publishing Company, Second Printing 1983, p. 79

27. Sweeten, Colen. "Moroni Timbimboo Interview," Provo: Charles Redd Center for Western Studies, Brigham Young University Oral History Project, 1970, p. 2

28. Parry, Mae. "The Northwestern Shoshone" in *A History of Utah's American Indians*, Forrest S. Cuch, editor. Salt Lake City: Utah State Division of Indian Affairs / Utah State Division of History, 2000, p. 35

29. Hart, Newell. *The Bear River Massacre*, Preston: Cache Valley Newsletter Publishing Company, Second Printing 1983, p. 104

30. *Sacramento Daily Union*, February 17, 1863 (Cited in Hart, Newell. *The Bear River Massacre*, Preston: Cache Valley Newsletter Publishing Company, Second Printing 1983, p. 103)

31. Sweeten, Colen. "Moroni Timbimboo Interview," Provo: Charles Redd Center for Western Studies, Brigham Young University Oral History Project, 1970, p. 2

32. Parry, Mae. "The Northwestern Shoshone" in *A History of Utah's American Indians*, Forrest S. Cuch, editor. Salt Lake City: Utah State Division of Indian Affairs / Utah State Division of History, 2000, p. 36

33. P. Edw. Connor, Official Report, February 6, 1863. (Cited in Hart, Newell. *The Bear River Massacre*, Preston: Cache Valley Newsletter Publishing Company, Second Printing 1983, p. 82)

34. Danielsen, Marie, compiler. *The Trail Blazer: History of the Development of Southeastern Idaho*, Daughters of the Pioneers, 1930, p. 12

35. Simmonds, A.J. "Looking Back: A first-hand account of the Battle of Bear River," *The Herald Journal/Valley*, Logan, Utah, April 9, 1979, p. 3

36. *The Evening Bulletin*, San Francisco, February 20, 1863. (Cited in Hart, Newell. *The Bear River Massacre*, Preston: Cache Valley Newsletter Publishing Company, Second Printing 1983, p. 94)

37. *The Sacramento Daily Union*, February 12, 1863. (Cited in Hart, Newell. *The Bear River Massacre*, Preston: Cache Valley Newsletter Publishing Company, Second Printing 1983, p. 99)

38. *The Deseret News*, February 11, 1863, p. 5

39. *The Alta California*, February 7, 1863 (Cited in Hart, Newell. *The Bear River Massacre*, Preston: Cache Valley Newsletter Publishing Company, Second Printing 1983, p. 111)

40. Official Report of P. Edw. Connor, February 6, 1863. (Cited in Hart, Newell. *The Bear River Massacre*, Preston: Cache Valley Newsletter Publishing Company, Second Printing 1983, p. 82)

41. 28. Parry, Mae. "The Northwestern Shoshone" in *A History of Utah's American Indians*, Forrest S. Cuch, editor. Salt Lake City: Utah State Division of Indian Affairs / Utah State Division of History, 2000, p. 37

42. *The Evening Bulletin*, San Francisco, February 20, 1863. (Cited in Hart, Newell. *The Bear River Massacre*, Preston: Cache Valley Newsletter Publishing Company, Second Printing 1983, p. 95)

43. Official Report of P. Edw. Connor, February 6, 1863. (Cited in Hart, Newell. *The Bear River Massacre*, Preston: Cache Valley Newsletter Publishing Company, Second Printing 1983, p. 84)

44. "The Bear River Massacre: New Historical Evidence" by Harold Schindler. *Utah Historical Quarterly,* Fall 1999, Volume 67, Number 4. p. 307

45. *Sacramento Daily Union*, February 17, 1863 (Cited in Hart, Newell. *The Bear River Massacre*, Preston: Cache Valley Newsletter Publishing Company, Second Printing 1983, pp. 105)

46. Parry, Mae. "The Northwestern Shoshone" in *A History of Utah's American Indians*, Forrest S. Cuch, editor. Salt Lake City: Utah State Division of Indian Affairs / Utah State Division of History, 2000, p. 37

47. Woonsock, Henry. "A Historical Tale Told To Lorin Gaarder, February 29, 1968," University of Utah, Western History Center, American Indian History Project, Doris Duke Number 352, p. 1-2

48. Simmonds, A.J. "Looking Back: A first-hand account of the Battle of Bear River," *The Herald Journal/Valley*, Logan, Utah, April 9, 1979, p. 3

49. "The Bear River Massacre: New Historical Evidence" by Harold Schindler. *Utah Historical Quarterly*, Fall 1999, Volume 67, Number 4, p. 307

50. *Sacramento Daily Union*, February 12, 1863 (Cited in Hart, Newell. *The Bear River Massacre*, Preston: Cache Valley Newsletter Publishing Company, Second Printing 1983, p. 99)

51. Parry, Mae. "The Northwestern Shoshone" in *A History of Utah's American Indians*, Forrest S. Cuch, editor. Salt Lake City: Utah State Division of Indian Affairs / Utah State Division of History, 2000, p. 37

52. Official Report of P. Edw. Connor, February 6, 1863. (Cited in Hart, Newell. *The Bear River Massacre,* Preston: Cache Valley Newsletter Publishing Company, Second Printing 1983, p. 82)

53. "The Bear River Massacre: New Historical Evidence" by Harold Schindler. *Utah Historical Quarterly*, Fall 1999, Volume 67, Number 4, p. 307

54. Simmonds, A.J. "Looking Back: A reminiscence of the Battle of Bear River," *The Herald Journal/Valley*, Logan, Utah, August 20, 1979, p. 3

55. "The Bear River Massacre: New Historical Evidence" by Harold Schindler. *Utah Historical Quarterly*, Fall 1999, Volume 67, Number 4, p. 307

56. Parry, Mae. "The Northwestern Shoshone" in *A History of Utah's American Indians*, Forrest S. Cuch, editor. Salt Lake City: Utah State Division of Indian Affairs / Utah State Division of History, 2000, pp. 38-39

57. William G. Nelson Diary (Cited in Hart, Newell. *The Bear River Massacre*, Preston: Cache Valley Newsletter Publishing Company, Second Printing 1983, p. 129)

58. Danielsen, Marie, compiler. *The Trail Blazer: History of the Development of Southeastern Idaho*, Daughters of the Pioneers, 1930, p. 13

59. Simmonds, A.J. "Looking Back: A first-hand account of the Battle of Bear River," *The Herald Journal/Valley*, Logan, Utah, April 9, 1979, p. 3

60. Madsen, Brigham D. *The Shoshoni Frontier and the Bear River Massacre*, Salt Lake City: University of Utah Press, 1985, p. 193

61. *Franklin County Citizen*, July 11, 1918

62. Parry, Mae. "The Northwestern Shoshone" in *A History of Utah's American Indians*, Forrest S. Cuch, editor. Salt Lake City: Utah State Division of Indian Affairs / Utah State Division of History, 2000, p. 42

63. Sweeten, Colen. "Moroni Timbimboo Interview," Provo: Charles Redd Center for Western Studies, Brigham Young University Oral History Project, 1970, p. 3

64. Official Report of P. Edw. Connor, February 6, 1863. (Cited in Hart, Newell. *The Bear River Massacre*, Preston: Cache Valley Newsletter Publishing Company, Second Printing 1983, p. 84)

65. *Sacramento Daily Union*, February 17, 1863 (Cited in Hart, Newell. *The Bear River Massacre*, Preston: Cache Valley Newsletter Publishing Company, Second Printing 1983, p. 106)

66. *The Deseret News*, February 11, 1863, p. 5

67. Madsen, Brigham D. *The Shoshoni Frontier and the Bear River Massacre*, Salt Lake City: University of Utah Press, 1985, pp. 190-192

68. "The Bear River Massacre: New Historical Evidence" by Harold Schindler. *Utah Historical Quarterly*, Fall 1999, Volume 67, Number 4, p. 307

69. Madsen, Brigham D. *The Shoshoni Frontier and the Bear River Massacre*, Salt Lake City: University of Utah Press, 1985, pp. 189-192

70. Official Report of P. Edw. Connor, February 6, 1863. (Cited in Hart, Newell. *The Bear River Massacre*, Preston: Cache Valley Newsletter Publishing Company, Second Printing 1983, p. 84)

71. McPherson. Robert S. *Staff Ride Handbook for the Battle of Bear River—29 January 1863*, Riverton: Utah National Guard, p. 58

72. Madsen, Brigham D. *Chief Pocatello*, Moscow: University of Idaho Press, 1999, p. 55

73. Parry, Mae. "The Northwestern Shoshone" in *A History of Utah's American Indians*, Forrest S. Cuch, editor. Salt Lake City: Utah State Division of Indian Affairs / Utah State Division of History, 2000, p. 42

74. Interview with Patty Timbimboo Madsen, secretary of the Northwestern Band of the Shoshone Nation, Brigham City, Utah, March 31, 2006

75. *The Deseret News*, February 11, 1863, p. 5; also in Connor's official report

76. *Franklin County Citizen*, July 11, 1918

77. Parry, Mae. "The Northwestern Shoshone" in *A History of Utah's American Indians*, Forrest S. Cuch, editor. Salt Lake City: Utah State Division of Indian Affairs / Utah State Division of History, 2000, p. 43

78. *Sacramento Daily Union*, February 17, 1863 (Cited in Hart, Newell. *The Bear River Massacre*, Preston: Cache Valley Newsletter Publishing Company, Second Printing 1983, p. 107)

79. Danielsen, Marie, compiler. *The Trail Blazer: History of the Development of Southeastern Idaho*, Daughters of the Pioneers, 1930, p. 13

80. *The Deseret News*, February 4, 1863, p. 5

81. *Sacramento Daily Union*, February 13, 1863 (Cited in Hart, Newell. *The Bear River Massacre*, Preston: Cache Valley Newsletter Publishing Company, Second Printing 1983, p. 101)

82. Madsen, Brigham D. *The Shoshoni Frontier and the Bear River Massacre*, Salt Lake City: University of Utah Press, 1985, p. 196

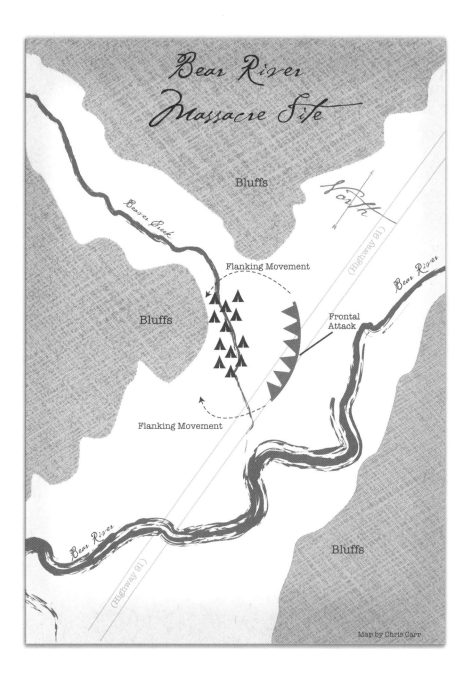

Map by Chris Carr

Chapter Five
MASSACRE AFTERMATH

These miscreants have been too long allowed to wanton in murder and robbery. They must finally be wiped out—it can be readily done—might have been done ere now, and should no longer be postponed. — Union Vedette, August 31, 1864

In short, Lo is being cultivated by the bloody priests, and that nation of red skin marauders...is being organized by the Mormon priesthood; and thus the good work done by Government, through Gen. Connor, is being all undone by Brigham Young. — Salt Lake Tribune, August 18, 1875

Shall there be an Indian war in a city and the Indians know nothing about it? Shall the doughty Corinnites be scalped to a man and the red skins be totally oblivious of the hairlifting enormity?— Deseret News, August 18, 1875

Both the military and the Mormons viewed the Bear River Massacre as cause for celebration.

The California Volunteers were unflinching in their enthusiasm. At a full-dress burial ceremony for those killed in the engagement, Colonel Connor ordered his adjutant to read out his report to General Wright, Commander of the Pacific Department. Connor praised the troops for their "brilliant victory" and said

"The gallant officers and men who were engaged in this battle . . .merit the highest praise."[1]

Even as Connor praised those under his command, his commanders heaped praise upon him. The most significant notice came in a March 29, 1863 telegram from Henry W. Halleck, General-in-Chief of the United States Army. "I congratulate you, and your command on the heroic conduct and brilliant victory on Bear River. You are this day appointed a Brigadier-General."[2]

Mormon reaction, while more tempered and less uniform, also tended to praise the outcome of Connor's expedition. A Franklin man said the Army's victory resulted from the "intervention of our heavenly Father," a woman in Wellsville called it "an interposition of providence," while a man in Logan believed that God had sent Connor "to punish them [the Indians] without us having to do it."[3]

A congregation of Saints in Logan recorded in official minutes a belief in the fight "as an intervention of the Almighty." Peter Maughan, however, introduced what can be read as a note of uncertainty among the claims of divine approval, along with his fear that the Cache Valley Mormons might be in line for a portion of blame for the massacre, when he opened his rationalization of his—and the settlers'—role saying, "I feel my skirts clear of their blood."[4]

No one asked, or no one recorded, Shoshoni views at the time.

❋❋❋

Expectations in the aftermath of the Bear River Massacre seem as confused as reports of the fight itself.

"The chiefs Pocatello and San Pitch, with their bands of murderers, are still at large," Colonel Connor wrote a few weeks after his triumphant return to Camp Douglas. While acknowledging the Shoshoni threat had not been eliminated, he expressed confidence it soon would be with the killing or capture of those chiefs and their bands, eradicating once and for all "the bedouins" who yet stood in the way of western travel.[5]

The *Deseret News*, too, said "conjecture leads to the conclusion that the end of the expedition has not yet come," and would not, until Connor either made "an end of Po-ca-tello and San Pitch" or drove their bands permanently away from emigrant trails.[6]

While acknowledging some mop-up may be required farther north, one California newspaper said that those who knew them best "think that the Indians will never again attempt a fair stand-up fight."[7]

The *New York Times* questioned the very wisdom of Connor's approach, believing a "conciliatory course" might have been better. The Easterners doubted the Indians had been "awed into good behavior" by the Volunteers. The opinion at the *Times* was that the Shoshoni, now "in no very amiable mood," would not take the fight to the troops at Camp Douglas; rather, Mormon settlements and emigrants on the plains "will feel the weight of Indian wrath."[8]

But many in those very Mormon settlements voiced enthusiasm for Connor's work and the expected results.

One Cache Valley man recorded in his journal that the massacre "put a quietus upon the Indians."[9] A local history, while calling it "one of the apparent barbarisms which history has to record" also records its importance, "as it marked the close of the real Indian troubles in this part of the territory."[10] Another voluminous history says "the defeat completely broke the power and spirit of the Indians, and the result was immediately felt throughout Northern Utah." Not only were settlements in Cache Valley thereafter secure, even the "flocks and herds were now comparatively safe."[11]

As it happened, the distant view of the *New York Times* proved clearest, at least for the short term.

Springtime, 1863, brought increased threats, violence, and retaliation from the shattered bands of Northwestern Shoshoni.

Sagwitch and San Pitch assembled raiding parties of survivors and recruits from bands farther north, "determined to steal every horse [they] can from settlers or travelers." Those traveling the Montana road felt unsafe amid reports that the Shoshoni intended to "make good their losses." In May, Mormon settlers gathering wood in a canyon near Franklin were attacked by a group of Shoshoni who threatened to "kill every white man they could" and, reportedly, "to steal some of the Mormon women." About that same time, Sagwitch and some of his followers stole a Mormon horse herd from a village farther south in Cache Valley. The Shoshoni leader soon returned the horses and spent a few days in custody. Peter Maughan, chronicling the incident for Brigham Young, claimed the raid was "retaliation for the Mormons helping the soldiers at Bear River last winter" and said he was "compelled to admit they have reason to feel bad." Other reports of vengeance, from harassment to murder to livestock rustling, came from Sardine Canyon, Brigham City, Ogden Valley, and neighboring areas and continued into June.[12]

❧❦❧❦❧❦❧

While the Northwestern Shoshoni rampaged through Cache Valley and elsewhere in northern Utah, the California Volunteers were distracted by troublesome Ute, Gosiute, and Shoshoni attacks south and west of Salt Lake City. Not only that, Colonel Connor and Brigham Young ratcheted up tensions between the Mormons and the military.

On March 12, Connor told his superiors at the Department of the Pacific that Young, apparently fearing attack from Camp Douglas, had called up and armed some 1,500 militia troops, dismissed most of them soon after, but kept patrols active throughout the city. A few days later, in a lengthy dispatch to California headquarters, the Colonel again reiterated his belief that the Mormons were disloyal to the Union, guilty of treason, and that they refused to submit to the law. Additionally, he reported the Saints were actively arming themselves in order to intimidate federal officers and the troops. While not believing his command in "immediate danger," Connor said he would "strike at the heads of the church" if the Mormons did not behave.[13]

A few weeks later, Young again assembled hundreds of Nauvoo Legion guards at his residence when cannon fire from the military camp up the hill shredded his nerves. As it turned out, the eleven blasts that echoed from Camp Douglas the three miles down Brigham Street were but a salute to honor Connor's promotion to Brigadier-General.[14]

In an attempt to kill two birds with one stone, The Volunteers again sent forces northward in May to establish a presence on the California-Oregon Trail at Soda Springs. The soldiers pitched their tents 150 miles north of Salt Lake City, forty-five miles upstream from the massacre site on the Bear River, and called the place Camp Connor. The soldiers' presence was intended to prevent Indian attacks against emigrants, as well as protect a colony of 160 expelled Mormons who accompanied the troops on the journey. Adherents to a crumbled apostate sect and survivors of the so-called Morrisite War with the Mormons the previous summer, the excommunicated Saints no longer felt safe in their former homes on the Weber River and sought the General's protection. He hoped—and fully expected—the settlement would be a magnet for disaffected followers of Brigham Young. The military camp would last little more than a year.[15]

Connor and Young continued to trade threats and insults, and hostilities were seldom far below the surface until the General mustered out of the Army in 1866. Even then, he stayed in Utah as a civilian for years afterward, continuing his self-assigned role as thorn in the Mormon side.

While the general never did come to terms with the Saints, he did, during the summer of 1863, play a role in attempts at peace making with the Shoshoni.

123

Political boundaries created by the United States government in Shoshoni country bore no resemblance to tribal reality. Homelands and migratory patterns routinely carried the Northwestern Shoshoni in and out of and back and forth between lands variously assigned to the political Territories of Utah, Oregon, Washington, Idaho, and Nevada.

This resulted, among other things, in confusion over responsibility for the Indians, ignorance—based partly on distance—about their circumstances, ambivalence in seeking and distributing aid, as well as uncertainty about treating with the Shoshoni.

So it was that James Doty, Superintendent of Indian Affairs in Utah Territory (who would be named Governor within a month), traveled with General Connor in May, 1863, on his mission to establish Camp Connor on the Bear River at Soda Springs. Doty's purpose was to meet with Shoshoni leaders at Fort Hall— in Washington Territory—seek peace, and warn that attacks on emigrants and settlers would result in "the most summary punishment, even to extermination."[16]

With assistance from the military, Doty traveled widely among the Shoshoni following the Fort Hall visit, and, through the summer and fall, negotiated a number of treaties. In a November 10, 1863 report to William C. Dole, Commissioner of Indian Affairs in Washington, D.C., Doty recounted his actions.

More than a thousand Eastern Shoshoni, representing three to four thousand of their people—"nearly the whole nation"— gathered at Fort Bridger in early July and signed a treaty "for the benefit of all the bands of the Shoshones nation who might give their assent."

A "Treaty concluded at Box Elder on the 30th of July" sought peace on the many roads through the country, including those to Montana mines, southern Oregon, and northern

124

California. Pocatello and San Pitch signed, along with leaders of other Shoshoni bands. Among them, according to Doty, were representatives of Bear Hunter's band, although "All but seven of this band were killed at the Bear River Battle." Sagwitch, he said, had been shot and wounded by a white man a few days before and could not attend or sign the treaty "but he assented to all of its provisions."[17]

Those provisions included a promise of amicable relations, agreement with the terms of the July 2, 1863 Fort Bridger treaty, a $5,000 annuity, $2,000 in goods at signing, and delineation of the borders of the country claimed by Pocatello and his people.

Doty also came to terms with Western Shoshoni at Ruby Valley on October 1, Gosiutes at "Tuilla Valley" October 12, and on October 14 at Soda Springs with "mixed Bands of Shoshonees and Bannacks."

"The whole number of Shoshonees, Goaships, and Bannacks who are parties to these Treaties," Doty reported, "may be estimated at Eight Thousand Six Hundred and Fifty."[18]

At the same time he aided Doty in his efforts to make peace with the Shoshoni, Connor was aggravated by continuing attacks on the trails and Indian difficulties elsewhere in the Territory.

Just before Connor's trip to Fort Hall in May, an April clash between a detachment of Volunteers and Little Soldier's band of Northwestern Shoshoni (called Weber Utes) near the abandoned Camp Floyd in Cedar Valley stretched over several days and many miles. It all ended with a protracted battle with a separate band of Utes in Spanish Fork Canyon, which the troopers encountered while chasing Little Soldier's band. In a series of related skirmishes along the Wasatch Front, one soldier and some thirty Indians were killed. (Not counting four army mules the soldiers blasted to hell with howitzer fire near the town of Pleasant Grove.)[19]

Along the overland trail westward, Volunteer forces responded to violent Indian attacks on mail carriers, stagecoaches, and other travelers through the spring and summer. The bloodiest battles resulted in the death of fifty-three Gosiutes in May, ten Indians left dead near Government Springs in Utah's west desert in June, and twelve Gosiutes killed near Schell Creek Station. The Indians took a measure of revenge at Canyon Creek Station, killing the agent and four soldiers. Despite his willingness to punish Indians, including reports of orders to "shoot all Indians," Connor blamed Mormons in disguise for most of the attacks and for otherwise instigating bad behavior among the tribes.[20]

But by October, with all the treaties signed, the General reported "peace with all the Indians in this military district," and that travel on the roads was "perfectly safe."[21]

Less than a year later, Connor and the California Volunteers once again rode out of Camp Douglas, this time in pursuit of Northwestern Shoshoni said to be interfering with travel on the Montana road and using stage stations as commissaries.

When representatives of the Overland Stage Line reported their displeasure to officials at Camp Douglas, Connor ordered the expedition northward to arrest Pocatello. The army commander did not bother with the niceties of informing the Indian agent, who was distressed to learn that if the general arrested the Shoshoni chief, he intended to "try him, and if guilty. . .hang him."[22]

Connor captured "The famous Snake Chief" and returned him to Salt Lake City for interrogation. The *Union Vedette* claimed the chief's bad behavior had "given him almost a national notoriety." The newspaper reported that Pocatello denied the accusations against him, and said he was "a pretty good Constitutional lawyer" as he refused to answer any questions "tending to incriminate himself." So, the report said, Connor informed the captive he would make further inquiries and if charges against him proved true, he would "hang him between Heaven and earth—a warning to all bad Indians."[23]

Apparently, stage line operator Ben Holladay and Doty's replacement as Superintendent of Indian Affairs, O. H. Irish, thought Connor's approach extreme, and that his true intention was to kill the hated Pocatello regardless of innocence or guilt. Both, too, feared that if Pocatello were killed, the Shoshoni would unleash a horrible war. Holladay wrote Connor that the charges against the chief were less serious than he had originally been told, and that punishment was unnecessary. Irish wired Washington D. C. asking the Commissioner of Indian Affairs to intervene, who went to the Secretary of the Interior, who went to President Lincoln, who told the Secretary of War to send Connor a telegram ordering him not to execute Pocatello. Which, as it turned out, was unnecessary as, by that time, the General had turned the chief over to Irish.[24]

Even as Pocatello's influence on military affairs reached eastward all the way to the White House, Connor's influence in Indian affairs reached eastward to the plains of Colorado and another killing field.

⁂

Arapaho, Cheyenne, and Sioux raiders went after Oregon Trail and Overland Mail traffic east of South Pass and southward into Colorado with a vengeance during the summer of 1864. Mail and stagecoach service ranged from sporadic to nonexistent, with several stations abandoned. A number of travelers and settlers were killed or captured by the raiders.

The Camp Douglas newspaper believed the miscreants should be "wiped out" and reminded authorities that the California Volunteers, "who have shown their capability in the Indian line of warfare at Bear River" were available and "would esteem it as a great satisfaction, could they be allowed the opportunity of wiping out the scoundrels."[25]

John Evans, governor of Colorado, must have shared that view to some extent, for he wired General Connor for assistance. Although champing at the bit, the General told the Governor he was powerless to act, as the troubles were outside his area of authority. So Evans and stage line operator Ben Holladay intervened in Connor's behalf with Army chief Henry W. Halleck in the nation's capital. Halleck gave the commander of the California Volunteers jurisdiction to protect the Overland Trail as far east as Fort Kearney in Nebraska "without regard to department lines."[26]

The zealous Connor soon overstepped his authority, confusing and upsetting army officers in the area, including Colonel John M. Chivington, Commander of the District of Colorado, about command structure and jurisdiction. Connor queried the Colorado commander about supplies and support for his expedition, and Chivington demanded to know from military authorities if there was a new link in the chain of command. He was assured otherwise. In any event, the point became moot in October when bad roads, bad weather, and bad forage forced Connor to abandon his planned march to Colorado, and the cavalry troops he intended to send to there instead went into winter quarters alongside some California Volunteer compatriots stationed at Fort Bridger.

Their commander, however, boarded an eastbound stage in November to make his presence felt in Denver. The General was feted at one of the city's finest hotels by Evans, Chivington, and a delegation of military, governmental, and civilian dignitaries, including a serenade by a military band. No doubt the two commanders engaged in a good deal of posturing during their time together, as both loved military trappings and pomposity with unusual ardor. They did exchange opinions about Indian fighting and the task facing Chivington, and Connor offered advice based on his experience at Bear River.

According to Chivington, Connor said the Colorado soldiers would likely "give these Indians a most terrible threshing if you catch them." The Brigadier suggested the best hope for success

would come in a situation similar to what he himself had faced—
if "you had them in a canon, and your troops at one end of it and
the Bear River at the other. . .but I am afraid on these plains you
won't do it." The Colorado commander disagreed. Connor told
Chivington to wire him in Salt Lake City "if you do catch them,"
then boarded the next westbound stage.[27]

On November 29, 1864, Chivington caught them.

Following Connor's example, he located a sleeping Indian
village blanketed by snow and attacked without warning at dawn.
When Chivington and his soldiers were finished with Black
Kettle's Cheyenne camp on Sand Creek, some 130 men, women,
and children lay dead. And, like the California Volunteers, the
Colorado soldiers tortured, raped, mutilated, and murdered Indians
in a savage frenzy.

And, like Bear River, some of the Indians punished at the Sand
Creek Massacre were most likely the wrong Indians.

⸎▦⸎▦⸎▦⸎▦

Chivington would not be the last military commander in the
Indian wars of the West to imitate Connor's vanguard tactics.

On the cold winter morning of November 27, 1868, George
Armstrong Custer and his cavalry troops charged out of the fog
to overwhelm a sleeping Cheyenne village on the Washita River
in Oklahoma. When the army rode away, they left more than 100
dead, mutilated Indians in the snow.

Major Eugene M. Baker followed suit, riding out in the dead
of winter in January, 1870. The army's ill-conceived attempt
to recover stolen mules prompted an attack on an undefended
Blackfeet village on the Marias River. One hundred and seventy-
three were killed, the majority of them women and children.

Colonel John W. Forsyth's troopers surrounded and disarmed
a captive camp of Lakota Sioux on Wounded Knee Creek in South
Dakota in the dawn light of December 29, 1890. In a cold-blooded

massacre triggered by chaos and confusion, nearly 150 mostly defenseless Indians died.

The United States Army, it seems, had taken note of Colonel Connor's cold-weather, cold-blooded strategy and tactics at Bear River.

In the years following the Bear River Massacre, Mormon immigrants continued to pour into Utah by the thousands. And all the while, the Saints continued their long-established Indian policy with the tribes who had occupied their Zion for centuries— an expressed desire to peacefully co-exist, accompanied by the practice of pushing the natives off any tract of land desirable for settlement, and destroying any who failed to comply.

The tribes, including the Northwestern Shoshoni, continued to suffer indirect consequences of the Mormon stampede as well. The wildlife, wild plants, water, and migration patterns upon which the Indians depended increasingly fell victim to guns, grazing, irrigation, and agricultural practices upon which the whites depended.

Still, after a bloody season of raids and retaliation in the months following the Bear River fight, the Shoshoni and Saints settled into a period of relative peace for the next several years. The peace was often tenuous, and occasionally violated, but serious troubles were, for the most part, avoided.

Their way of life rendered fragile in the circumstances, the Shoshoni were destitute—always short of food and frequently hungry. The Mormons in northern Utah were as generous with food as their circumstances allowed. Sagwitch and his people, who lived among the settlements more so than other bands, were frequently fed by Mormons. Pocatello often passed through Cache Valley and other mountain valleys occupied by the Mormons, and he and his people, too, usually left town better supplied than when they entered. And despite ongoing promises from the government to deliver food and annuities as guaranteed in the Fort Bridger and Box Elder treaties, the Mormons were a more reliable source of sustenance.

The peace in northern Utah held, even in the face of Indian difficulties in other parts of the Territory, including the drawn-out difficulties with Utes and Paiutes that comprised the Black Hawk War of 1865 and 1866. With the Mormon militia occupied in that conflict, an opportunistic alliance of renegade Shoshoni from Nevada and Fort Hall, and including some from Northwestern bands, encouraged Sagwitch to join forces with them and attack settlements in the Box Elder area and Cache Valley. He refused, and the plan disintegrated.

"I consider Sigewatch [Sagwitch] the most reliable Indian in this region," Mormon leader Peter Maughan wrote to his superiors in Salt Lake City upon hearing of the plan and the circumstances of its demise. "He has. . .prevented a collision between us and the Indians several times." The chief was also instrumental in protecting Brigham Young and his entourage from angry Indians during a visit to his flock in the northern settlements.[28]

Next came the establishment of the Fort Hall Indian Reservation in 1867, and life changed significantly for most of the Northern Shoshoni. In addition to the Fort Hall band already living along the Snake River in eastern Idaho, the government moved the Boise, Bruneau, and Lemhi bands to the reservation. Bannock bands in the area, too, were forced onto the Fort Hall Reservation.

Eventually, many people of the Northwestern bands took up residence there as well. But since the Box Elder Treaty afforded them the opportunity to continue living in country that had long been part of their traditional homelands, some opted to stay in Cache Valley and surrounding areas.[29]

Then, in 1869, the completion of the transcontinental railroad joined East and West at Promontory Summit, in the heart of Northwestern Shoshoni territory. Immigration increased with the arrival of the rails. Not only did Mormons arrive in greater

131

numbers, but the rails also attracted thousands of "Gentiles." Both groups would again change the Shoshoni way of life—the Saints in ways previously unimagined by the Indians, the Gentiles in ways unimagined by the Mormons.

※※※※※

Gentiles, Shoshoni, and Saints in the Box Elder area reached a crisis in early August, 1875.

"Mormons Meddling with the Indians!" the *Corinne Mail* newspaper trumpeted on August 9; "Mountain Meadows to be Repeated!!" The anti-Mormon sheet predicted a "Night of Terror!!!" in its August 11 edition and called for army troops and armed citizens to wipe out an encampment of more than a thousand hostile Shoshoni some ten miles north of town.[30]

This collision of the three parties came at the end of a long and winding road. The crash was set in motion, in a sense, the day Corinne was settled. Founded by Gentile squatters in February of 1869 at the site of an anticipated railroad crossing on the Bear River, the town sprouted on the west side of the stream just north of where it pours into the Great Salt Lake, some sixty miles from Salt Lake City. The hopefuls who founded the place initially called it Connor City after Utah's leading anti-Mormon. But by March, money men with bigger dreams of capitalizing on the coming railroad and dominating the Montana trade took over the town site and re-christened it Corinne.[31]

While the town never realized the Gentile dreams attached to it, either in terms of becoming a major trading center or in diluting Mormon control over Utah to the point of washing it out altogether, Corinne did thrive for a time. Then, in 1878, the new Utah Northern Railroad loaded up and hauled away the Montana trade, and the town all but died.

But, in the intervening years, Corinne was powerful enough to forever alter the history of the Northwestern Shoshoni.

In those days, too, their history would yet again be altered by the Church of Jesus Christ of Latter-day Saints—in a way the Mormons had hoped for but never expected, and which the Shoshoni could not have anticipated.

Since the earliest days of Mormonism, even before the foundation of the church, American Indians held a special place in the doctrine. According to the *Book of Mormon*, the blood of ancient Israel flowed through Indian veins. Indian realization and acceptance of their sacred history and future were considered important signs of the times; precursors to the glory of Zion and second coming of Christ. In all their relations with Indians, the Mormons were driven by the hope—the faith—that these long-lost emigrants from the Holy Land would see the light and embrace the gospel of the Latter-day Saints. At the same time, experience taught them not to expect it to happen anytime soon.

But in May of 1873 it happened.

There were no reports of angelic choirs and heraldic trumpets to mark the event, and conversions numbered in the hundreds rather than the thousands. But Shoshoni men, women, and children by the score suddenly entered the waters of baptism and emerged as Latter-day Saints, determined to change their lives to conform to the expectations of the Mormon religion.

George Washington Hill, or Inkapompy—"Man with Red Hair"—to the Shoshoni, had served among them at Fort Lemhi as a missionary in the late 1850s and, beginning in 1872, as a sort of assistant Indian agent and missionary headquartered in Ogden. Sagwitch showed up at Inkapompy's home one spring day in 1873 to say that the Great Spirit wanted his people to become Mormons, and "We want you to come to our camp and preach to us and baptize us."[32]

Hill did as asked, reporting that on May 7 he "baptized one hundred and two" of the Northwestern Shoshoni, about twenty on May 8, "and still they come and the work is extending like fire in the dry grass."[33]

133

The exuberant missionary continued his work among the Shoshoni for the next year. In late May of 1874, under instructions from Brigham Young, Hill and local Mormon leaders attempted to establish a permanent Indian settlement and farm near Franklin in northern Cache Valley, but abandoned the project by fall. So, in 1875, Hill, with Sagwitch's followers and Northwestern Shoshoni from other bands, tried again on the banks of the Bear River not far from Corrine. While Hill taught the Shoshoni to farm, he continued preaching and by early August reported 574 Indian baptisms.[34]

Neither the Shoshoni's newfound religion nor their newborn interest in agriculture impressed the citizens of Corinne. Already blinded by hostility toward the Saints, and with eyes squinted in anger over the recent acquittal of Mormon leader John D. Lee on charges related to the two-decades-old Mountain Meadows Massacre, the citizens saw nothing but threat in the large Indian encampment and its church sponsors.

So even as the newspaper stirred up fear and outrage in the town, city leaders demanded military support from Camp Douglas. The cavalry arrived August 11. Corinne's mayor, an interpreter, and Captain James Kennington set out for the Shoshoni village to confront Hill. The missionary reported on the affair for the *Deseret News*.

Hill's account has Kennington asking if reports of the threatened attack were true, and his own reply that "There is not a particle of truth in it." Point by point, Hill recounts the allegations and his refutation of them. He challenged the mayor to "give the name of any Indian" who threatened to attack the town or, go "through the camp, and you can point him out to me and I will have him at once fetched in and the matter forthwith investigated."

Despite finding no evidence to support any of the charges by Corinne's citizens, or anything to substantiate the possibility of an attack, Hill said an army major, newly arrived on the scene, came to the Shoshoni camp the following day and said "that all the Indians must leave the farm and go to their reservations before noon the next day, or he would be compelled to drive them therefrom by force."[35]

And so the Shoshoni decamped, leaving behind more than 125 acres of ripening wheat and vegetables they had barely begun to harvest.

The Mormons and their Shoshoni converts would continue attempts to establish farms in the area, eventually building, in 1881, a settlement they called Washakie. The town thrived until the 1940s and endured until 1960, when the last of the residents moved away, some under protest. Mormon officials, who wrongly considered the place abandoned, destroyed most of the remaining homes and sold the land the Shoshoni had long been led to believe would be theirs to use "in perpetuity."[36]

The Northwestern Band of the Shoshoni Nation later regained title to parts of the land, primarily a cemetery holding many Indian graves—including that of their chief Sagwitch. Once reported and memorialized as killed in the Bear River Massacre, the chief died and was buried at Washakie[37] in 1886 or 1887.[38]

***

Unlike Sagwitch, the Shoshoni who died years earlier in Beaver Creek ravine and along the banks of the Boa Ogoi knew neither grave nor cemetery. Left lying where they fell, the frozen bodies suffered the insult of scavenging creatures and the decay of time and weather.

"[At] the scene of Connor's battle with the ill fated Bear Hunter and his scallawag band of Northern braves," a *Deseret News* correspondent wrote in 1868, "The bleached skeletons of scores of noble red men still ornament the ground, and one can almost imagine he feels the influence of the departed still hanging around the battle field."[39]

If settlers in the area felt that influence they did not allow it to alter behavior. Rather than sanctify or hallow the ground, they plowed it. A small town, Battle Creek, grew up on the site in 1878, along the newly laid rails of the Utah Northern Railroad. But the town dwindled to only a few residents after 1886 when the roundhouse and later the tracks relocated, leaving the bottomland to farmers. When plows turned the soil on the massacre site, "quite a number of old relics were found, such as: old gun barrels, rusty knife blades, some human bones, bows and arrow heads." No one seemed to mourn much—"Circumstances alter cases," a local history reads. "Some places must yield to the march of progress."[40]

The march of progress makes today's landscape difficult to reconcile with descriptions of the massacre site. The Bear River follows a different meander pattern between the bluffs. Ditches, canals, roads, bridges, pole lines, fences, pastures, houses, haystacks, barns, and outbuildings scatter across the plain.

But the biggest change was wrought by floods sluicing mud and water down Beaver Creek ravine from the high ground above the bluffs. Triggered by deep snow, heavy rains, and a sudden thaw, the flood, worsened by waters from washed-out canals and an irrigation reservoir, was said to have covered the entire river bottom in 1911. "All that sand and silt and clay came pouring down the old battlefield," said a man who lived in Battle Creek. "Every bit of it is covered so that now it's hard to find a thing in the way of relics."[41]

So, when white men did not respect the remains of the Shoshoni and see to their interment, nature, it seems, did.

Chapter Five Notes

1. *Deseret News*, February 11, 1863, p. 5
2. Carter, Kate D., compiler. *Our Pioneer Heritage, Volume Six*. Salt Lake City: Daughters of Utah Pioneers, 1963, p. 125
3. Christensen, Scott R. *Sagwitch: Shoshone Chieftain, Mormon Elder. 1822-1887*. Logan: Utah State University Press, 1999, p. 58
4. Madsen, Brigham D. *The Shoshoni Frontier and the Bear River Massacre*. Salt Lake City: University of Utah Press, 1985, p. 194
5. U.S. Congress, House, *The War of the Rebellion*, vol. L, part I, p. 187 (cited in Madsen, Brigham D. *Chief Pocatello*. Moscow: University of Idaho Press, 1999, pp. 55-56)
6. *Deseret News*, February 11, 1863, p. 5
7. *Alta California*, February 7, 1863. (Cited in Hart, Newell. *The Bear River Massacre*. Preston: Cache Valley Newsletter Publishing Company, Second Printing 1983, p. 112)
8. *The New York Times*, February 25, 1863, p. 1
9. Christensen, Scott R. *Sagwitch: Shoshone Chieftain, Mormon Elder, 1822-1887*. Logan: Utah State University Press, 1999, p. 58
10. Danielsen, Marie, compiler. *The Trail Blazer: History of the Development of Southeastern Idaho*. Daughters of the Pioneers, 1930, p. 15
11. Bancroft, Hubert Howe. *History of Utah, 1540-1886*. San Francisco: The History Company, 1889, p. 632
12. Christensen, Scott R. *Sagwitch: Shoshone Chieftain, Mormon Elder, 1822-1887*. Logan: Utah State University Press, 1999, pp. 60-63
13. Hance, Irma Watson, complier. *Johnston, Connor, and the Mormons: An Outline of Military History in Northern Utah*. Salt Lake City: privately published, 1962, pp. 44-48
14. Carter, Kate D., compiler. *Our Pioneer Heritage, Volume Six*. Salt Lake City: Daughters of Utah Pioneers, 1963, p. 125
15. Madsen, Brigham D. *Glory Hunter: A Biography of Patrick Edward Connor*. Salt Lake City: University of Utah Press, 1990, p. 97
16. Madsen, Brigham D. *The Shoshoni Frontier and the Bear River Massacre*. Salt Lake City: University of Utah Press, 1985, p. 203-204
17. Carter, Kate D., compiler. *Our Pioneer Heritage, Volume Six*. Salt Lake City: Daughters of Utah Pioneers, 1963, pp. 126-127
18. Carter, Kate D., compiler. *Our Pioneer Heritage, Volume Six*. Salt Lake City: Daughters of Utah Pioneers, 1963, p. 127
19. Madsen, Brigham D. *The Shoshoni Frontier and the Bear River Massacre*. Salt Lake City: University of Utah Press, 1985, p. 205-206
20. Madsen, Brigham D. *The Shoshoni Frontier and the Bear River Massacre*. Salt Lake City: University of Utah Press, 1985, p. 208-209
21. Madsen, Brigham D. *Glory Hunter: A Biography of Patrick Edward Connor*. Salt Lake City: University of Utah Press, 1990, p. 98
22. Madsen, Brigham D. *Chief Pocatello*. Moscow: University of Idaho Press, 1999, p. 61
23. *Union Vedette*, October 27, 1864, p. 2
24. Madsen, Brigham D. *Chief Pocatello*. Moscow: University of Idaho Press, 1999, pp. 62-64
25. *Union Vedette*, August 31, 1864, p. 2
26. Madsen, Brigham D. *Glory Hunter: A Biography of Patrick Edward Connor*. Salt Lake City: University of Utah Press, 1990, p. 119
27. *Denver Republican*, May 18, 1890. Transcription provided by Jeff C. Campbell
28. Christensen, Scott R. *Sagwitch: Shoshone Chieftain, Mormon Elder, 1822-1887*. Logan: Utah State University Press, 1999, pp. 69-70
29. Madsen, Brigham D. *The Northern Shoshoni*. Caldwell: The Caxton Printers, 1980, pp. 49-52

137

30. Madsen, Brigham D. *The Northern Shoshoni*. Caldwell: The Caxton Printers, 1980, pp. 97

31. Madsen, Brigham D. *Corinne: The Gentile Capital of Utah*. Salt Lake City: Utah State Historical Society, 1980, pp. 5-9

32. Christensen, Scott R. *Sagwitch: Shoshone Chieftain, Mormon Elder, 1822-1887*. Logan: Utah State University Press, 1999, pp. 84-85, 87-88

33. Christensen, Scott R. *Sagwitch: Shoshone Chieftain, Mormon Elder, 1822-1887*. Logan: Utah State University Press, 1999, pp. 90-91

34. Madsen, Brigham D. *The Northern Shoshoni*. Caldwell: The Caxton Printers, 1980, pp. 96

35. *Deseret News*, September 1, 1875, p. 5

36. Parry, Mae. "The Northwestern Shoshone" in *A History of Utah's American Indians*. Forrest S. Cuch, editor. Salt Lake City: Utah State Division of Indian Affairs / Utah State Division of History, 2000, p. 58

37. Sweeten, Colen. "Moroni Timbimboo Interview," Provo: Charles Redd Center for Western Studies, Brigham Young University Oral History Project, 1970, p. 3

38. Christensen, Scott R. *Sagwitch: Shoshone Chieftain, Mormon Elder, 1822-1887*. Logan: Utah State University Press, 1999, p. 186

39. *Deseret News*, May 20, 1868, p. 5

40. Danielsen, Marie, compiler. *The Trail Blazer: History of the Development of Southeastern Idaho*. Daughters of the Pioneers, 1930, pp. 51-52

41. Hart, Newell. *The Bear River Massacre*. Preston: Cache Valley Newsletter Publishing Company, Second Printing 1983, pp. 117-118

Chapter Six

FORGETTING BEAR RIVER

If it wasn't the worst cavalry massacre of Indians in the country—east or west—it was certainly the most obscure, or obscured. — Newell Hart, Historian

Had the savages committed this deed, it would pass into history as a butchery or a massacre.— Hubert Howe Bancroft, Historian

Dead spirits are crying around there, they have not had a proper burial. — Lealand Pubigee, Shoshoni Leader

How do you explain the disappearance of an event as momentous as the Bear River Massacre? Why did the first and the worst of the Indian massacres in the West fade into obscurity, even as lesser incidents of a similar nature find and maintain prominence in the chronicles of history?

As is often the case in the study of causes and events, there is no simple answer. There are suggestions, opinions, speculations, ideas. But none is satisfactory, and even in sum, the explanations seem inadequate.

Whatever the reasons, few with even a passing familiarity of the tragedy would argue that the Bear River Massacre has taken its proper place in Western history. The precedent-setting attack on the Shoshoni winter camp on the *Boa Ogoi* established strategies and tactics that other armies would follow. And it set

139

a standard for butchery, mutilation, infanticide, rape, slaughter of noncombatants, and cold-blooded savagery that others would imitate in the Indian wars of the West but no one would equal.

Yet many have never heard of it. Most know little or nothing about it. Even among historians and scholars, most possess only scraps of awareness and snippets of knowledge.

Why?

What happened—or did not happen—in the aftermath of the Bear River Massacre and in the years since to relegate this extraordinary confrontation to the footnotes of history?

One explanation may be the near-total lack of footnotes. There has been relatively little scholarly study of the Bear River Massacre. Popular historians have largely ignored it. Even the novelists, poets, filmmakers, and artists have failed to give it notice. A basic search of the subject in the Library of Congress online catalog turned up only seven titles, some of which are limited in scope or purpose.

Of the few that treat the incident in detail, one is a self-published work by Newell Hart, a journalist and amateur historian who spent many years living and working in Idaho near the massacre site. Studying the massacre was his hobby; one to which he devoted countless hours of research and study, compiling documents and reports and accounts from sources throughout the West. His work is a helpful compendium, but the book was printed only in small limited editions, was never in general circulation, and is long out of print and difficult to find outside a few libraries and archives.

Three of the titles listed—two books and a paper—are the work of Brigham D. Madsen. Madsen, a pioneering historian, started delving into Indian history when few, if any, others thought it a subject worth pursuing. In fact, when Madsen told his graduate-school advisor at the University of California-Berkeley in 1946 of his plan to write his dissertation on the Bannock tribe of Idaho, he was told, "Don't. It's not important, not significant. There's no interest."

Madsen stubbornly pursued his interest, helping to launch the serious study of Indian history that flourished in decades to follow. He later served as tribal historian for the Shoshone-Bannock Tribes at Fort Hall, and spent hours and days in a damp cellar studying file case after file case of documents collected and mostly forgotten by the tribe over the better part of a century. In the process, he learned more, probably, about the details of the history of the Shoshoni than anyone else. His research proved essential to the tribes in a number of court cases, claims against the government, and other legal affairs.

His research also led to authorship of several books on the Shoshoni, including *The Shoshoni Frontier and The Bear River Massacre*, which he wrote, finally, "because no one else would."[1]

In that book, no doubt the most important to date on the subject, Madsen offers a brief opinion about the obscurity of the massacre. "The importance of the Bear River Massacre has been largely lost to history," he wrote, "because it happened during the Civil War when an obscure engagement with the Indians in far-off Utah became a minor incident compared to battles on the eastern front."[2]

His reasoning makes sense. Yet it seems inadequate as a full explanation.

While Civil War news surely dominated public forums in those days, it is worth noting there were no major events related to the Civil War that might have overwhelmed news of the Bear River Massacre. Union and Confederate forces clashed at Fredericksburg in mid-December, 1862. The Emancipation Proclamation took effect January 1, 1863, nearly a full month before Connor and his California Volunteers took on the Shoshoni encamped on Beaver Creek. And no major battle occurred in the War Between the States until Chancellorsville in May.

Too, if the Civil War alone was reason enough to doom the Bear River Massacre to a dusty corner shelf of American history, one would expect to find the Sand Creek Massacre right there beside it, similarly forgotten, likewise unknown.

But that is not the case.

Both occurred during the Civil War—Bear River in January, 1863; Sand Creek in November, 1864. Both happened in the remote West—Bear River at the edge of Utah Territory, Sand Creek on the isolated plains of Colorado.

Despite the similarities, the Sand Creek Massacre seems much better remembered. For instance, where the Library of Congress online catalog lists seven titles under the "Bear River Massacre" subject heading, a similar search for "Sand Creek Massacre" lists twenty-seven titles, in addition to others entries—eleven in total—in categories for Fiction, Juvenile Literature, Poetry, Drama, Historic Sites, and Antiquities. Simple arithmetic might lead one to believe the Sand Creek Massacre's importance is more than five times greater than the Bear River Massacre's.

This, surely, cannot be the case from the perspective of historical significance.

Even at the time, Sand Creek was seen through different eyes than Bear River. Within two months of his punishing the Shoshoni, the United States Army and civilian authorities in the government praised Colonel Connor and rewarded him with a promotion to Brigadier-General. Chivington, on the other hand, was roundly criticized in the press, by politicians, by the public, by military authorities. Unlike the reward Connor received, the Army's response to Chivington's victory was an investigation, which characterized the commander as "an inhuman monster." Chivington resigned his commission, but still endured the further embarrassment of more investigations by both houses of Congress, followed by more military inquiries in 1865.[3]

Just why Connor's expedition did not arouse the same ire, despite its equal savagery and higher body count, can only be guessed at. Had there been more outrage and fewer accolades, perhaps Bear River would be as famous today as Sand Creek.

Instead, federal officials in Utah supported it. Mormon leaders and newspapers either mildly criticized the affair, praised it, or attributed Connor's success to divine intervention on behalf of the settlers. The military hierarchy honored it.

Only the Shoshoni decried it, and no one listened.

The Bear River Massacre managed to fade from public consciousness—or fail to enter it—despite fairly widespread news coverage. Locally, the expedition and related events were well chronicled in the pages of the *Deseret News*, the weekly Mormon newspaper published in Salt Lake City.

Most of the ink on paper concerning the massacre, however, was pressed in California. The Salt Lake City newspaper, in fact, borrowed a goodly amount of its material on the expedition from those Golden State reports.

News of the California Volunteers' activities was of great interest in their home state, and the newspapers fed that interest with a great deal of coverage. The most extensive reporting was found on the pages of the *Sacramento Daily Union*, which published four lengthy articles on the massacre in its early February numbers. Bear River stories covered the pages of the metropolitan *San Francisco Evening Bulletin* by the foot; extensive coverage was also provided in the *Stockton Daily Independent*, *Alta California*, and newspapers in Napa and other localities.

And lest one assume that Easterners were not informed of the events on the banks of the *Boa Ogoi* that January morning, the *New York Times* filled an entire column, top to bottom, in the middle of page one on Wednesday, February 25, 1863.

A contributing factor to the forgetting, perhaps, was the massacre's location. It may be that the arbitrary manner political boundaries are created in the United States of America prevented

143

the massacre from ever gaining sufficient traction in any of the places it could have, should have.

The winter camp on the *Boa Ogoi* was, at the time of the attack, in Washington Territory. Physically, it was far, far away from governmental, military, civil, or any other kind of authority in that Territory. It is, perhaps, no surprise that Washington would little note the massacre in its history.

Then, within weeks of the massacre—on March 4, 1863—Idaho Territory was established, and the new political subdivision encompassed the killing field. So, while the blood-drenched soil was now called Idaho, that place did not even exist during the fight. And, again, political responsibility was far away—physically, culturally, and historically—in Boise. So while Idaho could not simply shed itself of the massacre as the previous landlord had, the reality is that it did not happen in Idaho.

All this is, of course, complicated by the presence of Utah. While many at the time believed the fight took place in Washington Territory, many others thought it was in Utah. That bit of confusion was not cleared up for a decade, when a formal survey officially established the border and forever fixed the massacre site in Idaho, never to wander again.

Invisible political boundaries aside, the reality was that all of Cache Valley was then, and is now, inextricably tied to Utah both culturally and economically. The same can be said for most of eastern Idaho. Having been settled by Mormons coming north out of, or being directed from, Salt Lake City, the Cache Valley looked south to Brigham Young for leadership and direction. And that applied to things economic, political, military, and civil as well as religious.

Beyond that, the connection is very real in a physical sense. Geographically and geologically, the Wasatch Range that hugs Salt Lake City and the valleys that flank it, stretches northward from Utah many miles across the Idaho border, the existence of which the landscape ignores. That a political boundary lops off the northernmost twenty-or-so miles of a Utah valley and assigns it to Idaho is physically illogical.

Indian agents, Mormon leaders, Connor, and the Shoshoni were all aware of the complications created by the imaginary line, wherever it was. Long-established migratory paths and settlement patterns dictated that the Northwestern Shoshoni, like the Mormon interlopers in their land, would naturally look southward for aid and assistance. Likewise, military discipline would come from federal troops stationed in the vicinity of Salt Lake City.

Still and all, when it comes right down to it, if you are Utah you are entitled to the fact that the Bear River Massacre did not happen there.

In some sense, then, the Bear River Massacre is something of an orphan. It can be genetically linked to three states as parents, none of which has embraced it—Washington has essentially ignored it, while Idaho and Utah have, at best, held it at arm's length.

Even the Shoshoni survivors and their descendants were split by the border. Some sought refuge with relatives near Fort Hall in Washington, then Idaho, and eventually assimilated into the Shoshone-Bannock society established there with the reservation. Others clung to a tenuous existence in their traditional homelands in Cache Valley, the Box Elder region, and surrounding areas.

Although recognized in the Box Elder Treaty of 1863, the Northwestern Band was largely ignored afterward by the federal government, often lumped with the Eastern Shoshone at the Wind River Reservation and the Shoshone-Bannock at the Fort Hall Reservation. Yet Congress added a provision to the Box Elder Treaty, Article 5, that limited the bands' claims to lands occupied when northern Utah belonged to Mexico; prior, that is, to 1848.[4] In limiting Northwestern Shoshoni rights to claim other land, their right to claim traditional land seems implicit.

And the people believed it so. Willie Ottogary, long-time Shoshoni correspondent with area newspapers, mentioned land rights in some of his dispatches. "I expect we going to have land allotted by Government pretty soon. Our people haven't got any land for their own," he wrote to a Logan, Utah, newspaper in April, 1928. "We have two Lawyers working on our case. But Northwestern Band Shoshone against United States, accordance the treaty June 30, 1863. We will win the case in future time. I expect going have a big reservation here at Bear River Valley, about year or two."[5]

⁂

Instead, rather than being recognized as a distinct band with rights to land or to compensation, the federal courts ruled in 1939 that the Box Elder Treaty of 1863 was of no more consequence than "a treaty of friendship." The band barely survived determined efforts by the federal government to "terminate" any kind of "special relationship" between them and the federal government in 1957. Thirty years later, the Bureau of Indian Affairs acknowledged the official formation, by vote, of the Northwestern Band of the Shoshone Nation.[6] With the move, the federal government extended—for the first time since 1863—a measure of recognition of the existence of a people it had all but wiped off the face of the earth that January morning on the banks of the *Boa Ogoi*.

⁂

But, back to the forgetting of the Bear River Massacre in the states where it should be remembered best: Idaho and Utah.

Idaho students learn the history of their state in eighth grade. Just how much class and textbook time the deadliest Indian massacre in Western history deserves is impossible to determine. Some Idaho schools, however, have determined that it doesn't deserve much.

One popular textbook covers the massacre only in a chronological list, where just over a single line of type mentions 300 to 400 Shoshoni deaths.[7] Another text gives it less than 300 words, less than half a page. Still, in that brief space, the book

146

manages to misspell Colonel Patrick Connor's name (Conner), incorrectly site the attack on the Montana miners at Battle Creek (which is several miles away from the actual location west of the Bear River west of Richmond), claim a body count of "300 Indian men and fifty Indian women and children." The narrative also fails to even mention that the conflict involved the Shoshoni, saying, instead, that the "battle crushed the power of the Bannock tribe."[8]

Utah's eighth graders are exposed to more information, or at least the opportunity for more exposure exists. The standard text for Utah history courses first mentions the Bear River Massacre on a timeline. Also included is a half-page photograph of the massacre site with locations of forces and movements marked, and about half a page of narrative. An "Activity Chart" invites students to record basic information for review purposes about the Bear River Massacre and four other conflicts with Indians in Utah. Another half page of text talks about the conversion of Sagwitch and many of his Northwestern Shoshoni followers to the Church of Jesus Christ of Latter-day Saints, and a sidebar features Sagwitch in a "Utah Portrait."[9]

Mormon-focused histories often include brief accounts of the massacre. But it was, after all, an affair between the hated California Volunteers and barely tolerated Indians. The Saints tend to portray themselves in their own histories as victims of Shoshoni depredations and innocent bystanders at the battle, and, afterward, rescuers of an ill-equipped army, saviors of wounded Shoshoni, and adopters of abandoned Indian children. All of which is true, to a certain extent, but too simplistic to serve as a realistic explanation or history.

Given tumultuous relationships between the Mormon church and mainstream America during the three decades leading up to the massacre and for at least another three decades afterward, it is perhaps understandable the Saints would be protective of their role in history.

This tendency is apparent in the account of the massacre chronicled in a comprehensive six-volume official history of the church. The narrative runs to just over 2,000 words; just shy of 900 of those words are taken up with refutations of Connor's accusations that the Saints were uncooperative, that his army was overcharged for supplies, that the Mormons were sympathetic with and supplied the Shoshoni, and such. In rebuttal, the author "cited the *Deseret News'* sympathetic account of the whole expedition both while forming, and also in recording its achievements."[10]

Much like the Walker War, the Black Hawk War, the Mountain Meadows Massacre, the Gunnison Massacre, and dozens of other blood-soaked episodes involving Indians in pioneer Deseret and Utah Territory, the Bear River Massacre is but a blip in Mormon history. While pageants and reenactments and parades commemorate the heroic overcoming of hardships, the desert blossoming as a rose through hard work, and the very survival of Zion on numerous occasions owing to miraculous occurrences, the slaughter of more than two hundred and fifty Shoshoni on a frozen battlefield near the northern frontier merits small note and little recognition in Mormon history.

⁂

The military maintained, as the military does, files and records of all the activities of the California Volunteers. Correspondence, reports, orders, rolls, lists, and all manner of minutiae are housed in military archives, published in various books, and many are posted online. But, while the records exist, they are but an insignificant molehill among the mountains of Civil War documentation.

Most military histories of the era focus on events in the East, which is understandable given the size and scope and severity of the conflicts there. One historian claims the "vast national literature" of the Civil War "simply ignored the events of the conflict in the western sections of the nation."[11]

After the Civil War, Indian battles in the West became big news. Officers from the War Between the States added luster to their careers and decorations to their uniforms fighting Indians Out West. New military heroes were minted. Indians—primarily the Plains tribes, such as the Sioux, Cheyenne, Comanche, Kiowa, and Arapaho—became household names. Crazy Horse, Sitting Bull, Geronimo, Chief Joseph, Quanah Parker, and other Indian leaders were well known, for good or ill, throughout the nation.

This, despite the fact that no tribe was responsible for as many emigrant deaths or depredations as the Shoshoni of earlier years. This, despite the fact that Bear Hunter, Pocatello, Lehi, San Pitch, and other Shoshoni chiefs who led the raids are essentially unknown. This, despite the fact that Patrick Edward Connor, the military officer responsible for killing more Indians in a single engagement than any other commander in Western history, is largely forgotten.

"If Connor's attack on Bear Hunter's village had occurred later, in the 1870s," Brigham D. Madsen contends, "Connor might not be the West's forgotten general." He goes on to write that Utah historians should "revise their bias toward Mormon history to include Indian troubles in the northern counties," and for historians studying the Indian wars in the post-Civil War era to review them "in light of early white-Indian interactions west of South Pass."[12]

One thing is certain: unless the historians who help us remember our past begin to remember the Bear River Massacre, it will remain forgotten.

Chapter Six Notes

1. Personal interviews with Brigham D. Madsen, March, 2006
2. Madsen, Brigham D. *The Shoshoni Frontier and the Bear River Massacre*. Salt Lake City: University of Utah Press, 1985, p. 222
3. Hoig, Stan. *The Sand Creek Massacre*. Norman: University of Oklahoma Press, 1961, pp. 163-169
4. Madsen, Brigham D. *The Shoshoni Frontier and the Bear River Massacre*. Salt Lake City: University of Utah Press, 1985, p. 212
5. Kreitzer, Matthew E., editor. *The Washakie Letters of Willie Ottogary*. Logan: Utah State University Press, 2000, p. 172
6. Parry, Mae. "The Northwestern Shoshone" in *A History of Utah's American Indians*. Forrest S. Cuch, editor. Salt Lake City: Utah State Division of Indian Affairs / Utah State Division of History, 2000, pp. 70-72
7. Thayer, Thomas N. and Murphy, Shar L. *Discovering Tomorrow Through Yesterday: Idaho History*. Billings: Northwest Speaks, 2001
8. Young, Virgil M. *The Story of Idaho*. Moscow: University Press of Idaho, 1977, pp. 126-127
9. Holzapfel, Richard Neitzel. *Utah: A Journey of Discovery*. Salt Lake City: Gibbs Smith, Publisher, 1999
10. Roberts, Brigham H. *Comprehensive History of Church of Jesus Christ of Latter-day Saints*. Volume 5, Chapter CXXI, Salt Lake City: Deseret News Press, 1938
11. Josephy, Alvin M., Jr. *The Civil War in the American West*. New York: Vintage Books, 1993, p. XI
12. Madsen, Brigham D. *The Shoshoni Frontier and the Bear River Massacre*. Salt Lake City: University of Utah Press, 1985, p. 222

Chapter Seven
REMEMBERING BEAR RIVER

The battle of Bear River was a great benefit to the settlers of Northern Utah. It gave the Indians a warning that did not have to be repeated. — Orson F. Whitney, Historian

In retrospect, the annihilation of the Northwestern Shoshoni at Bear River seems an unnecessary and extremely cruel action.— Brigham D. Madsen, Historian

The Bear River massacre site should be a place that is protected from any development that would harm its significant historic and sacred qualities. — United Sates Department of the Interior, National Park Service

While the Bear River Massacre is absent from our national consciousness, it did, for a time at least, establish a presence closer to home. Memories of the fight found their way into local folklore, family legends, community reminiscences, even heroic Mormon mythology.

And, just as caught fish tend to increase in size with each recounting of their capture, passed-down massacre tales exaggerate the incident in every imaginable direction. As imagination and embellishment took hold, spilled blood became redder, plunder was amplified, tortures grew more grotesque, proximity turned into participation, involvement developed out of observation.

151

Among the most fantastic distortions must be the insistence on the part of the United States Army to use the official designation "The Battle of Bear River" long after the true nature of the conflict was well known and documented. In 1977, more than a century after the brutality, the killing of noncombatant women, the slaughter of children, the rape, the arson, the other savagery, the word "Battle" was still part of the official military vocabulary in discussing the events of January 29, 1863.[1]

It took a concerted effort to persuade the military to change the designation. In particular, Brigham D. Madsen was instrumental in this drawn-out process. Madsen, himself, used the then-common designation "The Battle of Bear River" as a chapter title in his book *The Bannock of Idaho*, originally published in 1958.[2] But, additional research over the years changed his view. A memorial lecture delivered at a Utah college in 1983 under the title, "Encounter with the Northwestern Shoshoni at Bear River in 1863: Battle or Massacre?" issued a formal challenge.[3] Articles, books, and other lectures applied further pressure. Madsen, although not an especially popular figure around Fort Douglas, was invited to lecture there on Patrick Edward Connor, the installation's founder and subject of a biography by Madsen. While he tried to be even-handed, Madsen said many in attendance weren't pleased with his account because Connor was "not the hero they expected."[4]

Shoshoni historian Mae Timbimboo Parry wrote "many letters trying to get the name changed to massacre," she told a newspaper interviewer. "Sometimes I felt like the Lone Ranger."[5] When, in 1986, the state legislatures of Utah and Idaho jointly resolved to create a "Battle of Bear River Monument," she threatened suit on behalf of the Shoshoni to prevent use of the word "Battle."[6]

The 1997 publication of a document written by Sergeant William L. Beach of the California Volunteers provided a new eyewitness. In writing of the discovery, Harold Schindler said the document laid to rest any question of a massacre. In describing the fight, the sergeant told of soldiers breaking through Shoshoni defenses "into their very midst when the work of death commenced in real earnest." This moment, Schindler said, was fundamental: "Bear River began as a battle, but it certainly degenerated into a massacre."[7]

The efforts of Madsen, Parry, Schindler, and others eventually paid off. A high-ranking military officer representing Fort Douglas visited a council meeting of the Northwestern Band of the Shoshone Nation in 2002, finally, to announce the Army's intention to forever afterward use the designation "Bear River Massacre." Also, two large binders filled with copies of military documents related to the massacre were presented to the council.[8]

And so one memory—an important, official one—changed to more closely match the consensus of what actually happened and what it should be called.

There are other stories that, without official sanction, likewise distort—or, at least, present alternative views—of what happened on the *Boa Ogoi*. A Cache Valley historian collected dozens of such tales and published them in his book in a chapter titled "Apocrypha." He allowed that "Many may well be true," but they are "difficult, if not impossible to verify." Some, indeed, seem credible. Most disagree with the nature of other accounts. Still other tales are too outlandish to take seriously.

There are, for example, stories of Shoshoni disemboweling horses on the battlefield in order to warm hands or feet, even stuffing babies into the steaming cavity to prevent their freezing. Likewise, one supposed battlefield visitor claimed the only thing he remembered was a puppy seeking warmth in the entrails of a dead Indian.

An unfortunate Franklin woman was said to have reached into the pocket of a borrowed soldier's coat following the fight, and found a fresh scalp there. Another settler claimed to have overheard troopers saying, before the fight, "We'll have Indians for breakfast and Mormons for supper."

Connor, of course, was both glorified and vilified in massacre folklore. There were claims the Colonel did not allow women and children to be killed, but, in fact, protected them during the fight and provisioned them afterward. Other tales, though, told of his command to "kill everything you see—nits make lice."

Sagwitch was rendered heroic in one story; shot through both legs, he swam the Bear River's icy waters then crawled twenty miles through deep snow to the safety of Pocatello's lodge. Pocatello, on the other hand, was called a coward—reportedly seen astride his best horse riding away from the fight on the run.

The supposed role of various Mormons added a luster of gallantry to the affair. There were claims that "white men of conscience tried to stop the carnage." Apparently unsuccessful in their attempts to persuade the soldiers to kindness, the settlers hid women and children in the brush. One man is said to have used a lasso rope to rescue a mother and child, tangled in mud and branches, from drowning, then built a warming fire in the heat of battle to dry their clothes.[9]

The origin of many of the stories so collected and passed down is known; others seem to have sprung from nowhere. Most, it seems, serve to counter or reinforce biases and culturally acceptable attitudes surrounding the massacre.

A military commentator claimed the Shoshoni lured the soldiers to the Bear River fight "without a doubt" at the behest of the Mormons. The Mormons, "being unfriendly to our army thought they would betray us into the hands of the Indians," John Vance Lauderdale said in a letter. "They made the Indians believe they could capture us most easily & agreed to reward them finely if successful."[10] Lauderdale, an army surgeon, did not arrive in Utah Territory until more than a year after the massacre and reportedly "detested the Mormons."[11] It seems incredible that Colonel Connor, who eagerly accused the Saints of any crime or complicity or conspiracy he could conceive of or conjure, would miss such collusion.

One confused version attributed leadership of the expedition to Colonel Steptoe. (Brevet Lt. Col. Edward J. Steptoe wintered in Utah in 1854-55 with a herd of army mules and horses bound for the West Coast. He was later offered, but refused, the territorial governorship of Utah.[12]) While conforming roughly to certain details of the massacre, this autobiographical account—not an eyewitness account; the author said he lived in nearby Richmond at the time and talked to soldiers there on their return—claims 1,200 Indians killed and 1,500 ponies captured.[13]

Another Utah man said he learned from an eyewitness that it was the Shoshoni who crossed the ice-covered Bear River and attacked the soldiers. Six hundred Indians died, 400 escaped.[14]

Hans Jespersen (sometimes spelled Jasperson), a pioneer living in Goshen, Utah, said in a dictated biographical sketch in 1911, and wrote in a 1913 letter, that he visited the battlefield sometime after the massacre—just when is unclear, the letter says "early in spring"—while on a freighting expedition to either the Salmon River or Bannack, Montana. Jespersen says he "started to count dead Indians along the bank of the River and up the little creek. I counted 493 dead Indians. I turned around and counted them back and counted just the same." While aspects of his accounts indicate some knowledge of the incident, other facts—such as his claim that "the Indians had killed 60 men and wounded 60 more" and "The soldiers had killed all the Indians but two and they had got across the river"—depart from well-documented reports. Other information, such as his accompanying Lot Smith, a well-known Mormon and participant in the Utah War of 1857, to the battlefield, and his crossing "Bear River on the bridge close to Cache Valley" (there were only fords in Cache Valley at the time, no bridges) invite skepticism.[15]

Sylvanus Collett was another Utah pioneer who claimed to have witnessed the fight. A sometimes lawman, Collett, along with Porter Rockwell, was indicted some two decades after the fact for the 1857 murder of a party of California gamblers. He lived in Cache Valley in 1863 and a biographical sketch said he watched the massacre "from a nearby eminence." The Shoshoni were having the best of it, apparently, until "wicked fire from howitzers mounted on mules' backs ended the affray in the almost complete annihilation of the Indians."[16] Connor's artillery, however, was stuck in the snow several miles away and never did reach the massacre field.

And yet muleback mountain howitzers made an appearance in another personal account. This particularly gruesome story was attributed to Christian Garff, long-time Mormon resident of Cache Valley, who told his scribe he was "one of the members of Connor's Command." His tale, too, had the Shoshoni getting ripped apart by cannon fire. Two more hours of fighting followed, after which soldiers "stuck their bayonets through men, women, and children. Dead or alive." Garff listed "the heads of Bear Hunter and Pocatello" among items of plunder taken back to Camp Douglas. There, he said, he "had the pleasure of cooking the heads of these two chiefs until they were perfectly white and free from flesh, hair, and nothing left but the bone."[17]

Despite the documented lack of artillery on the field, such legends persisted. A 1978 feature story in a Logan, Utah, newspaper said that while the details of the battle were well known, "to date we have no record that the two field pieces lugged from Salt Lake through deep snow were brought in to play." True—but there *is* plenty of evidence that the howitzers were *not* brought into play. And yet the news story reported the finding, by metal detector, of "an artillery shell in the sandhills. . .northeast of the battle site." The author said the location of the round implied cannon fire may have covered the soldiers' pivotal flanking attack and, if the find proved authentic, it would change "our whole understanding of the battle."[18]

Another example of passed-down anecdotes comes from a purported participant in the Bear River Massacre who spent the most of the engagement stuck beneath a dead horse as bullets whizzed around him. The fight with "tribes of Sues and Arapahoes" started when the cavalry arrived at the river in the afternoon to see "700 or 800 Indians, all males. . .in the midst of a war dance." Once engaged, "It was a massacre on both sides," with sixty-five soldiers and hundreds of Indians killed.[19] Numerous other incidents inconsistent with accounts of better provenance fill out the trapped soldier's story.

Not all accounts that seem to vary from the norm came from Mormons or the military. The Shoshoni, too, related differing stories. One oral history, it appears, claimed that Shoshoni leaders would not allow women and children to leave the village as it came under attack. "You must stay with us because if you leave the rest will leave,"[20] the curious story goes.

Yeager Timbimboo, who survived the massacre as a young boy by hiding among the dead, disagreed with the generally accepted body counts, telling his son, "There ain't no two hundred Indians killed. There were less than that."[21] As noted before, Yeager's younger brother Be-shup (Frank Timbimboo Warner), who also survived the fight, estimated the Shoshoni dead at 156; seventy-three men, forty women, and forty-three children.[22]

Some Shoshoni memories blamed a shortage of men on the scene as the reason behind so much bloodshed. According to one story, the "hunters and young men went hunting" the day of the massacre, "to get some buffalo, elk, and deer meat to bring back to their loved ones to have a big celebration."[23] As a result, "when Colonel Connors came, when the men were hunting away from the campsite, and nobody was there, just the women, and so that's how come a lot of them were killed."[24]

<hr>

Folklore, legends, and myths were not the only means of remembering the Bear River Massacre. Celebrations, commemorations, and monuments also memorialized the attack on the Shoshoni winter camp.

"The first anniversary of the hard fought battle and glorious victory" was celebrated with all manner of festivities at Camp Douglas. In announcing the program, the *Union Vedette* reminded readers that "In that day's fight many a gallant soldier went down, and in honor of the dead and the living the celebration to-morrow will be held." A dress review and parade of soldiers before dignitaries, prayer, choral music, an oration, and band concert were listed on the "Order of Exercises."[25]

Captain Charles H. Hempstead delivered the oration, which was published in its colorful entirety in the anniversary edition of the newspaper. "The gallant deeds of our brethren in arms," "the shrill north wind. . .freezing with its cold breath every rivulet and stream," "the hot, raking, blazing fire of the protected red skins," "California's brave sons," "few of the savages escaped to tell the tale of the Battle of Bear River," "the spirits of the good and true have wended their flight," and other such florid phrases decorated the winter air. The same edition included a lengthy report of a voluntary monument fund established by the enlisted men for the design, construction, and placement of a twenty-foot-two-inch marker at Camp Douglas "to testify in a suitable manner the veneration and honor in which they held the memory of their fallen comrades."[26]

And still the celebrations continued. The next day's newspaper included the text of a "fine poetical production" written by E. T. Hingston and read by Mrs. S. M. Irwin in the Camp Douglas Theater. "Huzza! Now we have outflanked them / Quarter give nor mercy show;" it read in part, "Mercy would be heartless mock'ry with / your dark relentless foe." Yet another lengthy news report gushed about the gaiety of the Anniversary Ball.[27]

The *Union Vedette* reported no formal anniversary observance at Camp Douglas in 1865, owing to the "absence of Maj. Bull" who was "long delayed." Apparently the soldiers were disappointed, as "There is no event, which the men in this District enjoy celebrating so much."[28]

Reports of "perhaps the greatest cavalry feat on record" in the *Army and Navy Journal*—referring to an 1866 engagement between a Sioux war party and the Second U. S. Cavalry—drew a lengthy response to the editors of that publication; a reprint of which appeared in the Camp Douglas newspaper on the fourth anniversary of the Bear River Massacre. The correspondent recounted the 1863 battle and the heroic deeds of Connor and the California Volunteers, closing with the challenge, "Who can excel the battle of Bear River?"[29] The *Montana Post* later reprinted the account, claiming the Bear River fight "did not attract the attention East as it deserved,"[30] and was worthy of remembrance and recognition.

While the massacre faded from public consciousness in Utah Territory in the years to come—if published references are any indication—it certainly was not forgotten. In 1872 the *Salt Lake Tribune*, an anti-Mormon newspaper, took the pro-Mormon *Herald* to task in its pages when that paper took the federal government and army to task in its pages for their Indian policies. "In the first place, touching our Indian affairs" the *Tribune* said, "we will instance the famous battle of Bear River."[31] That newspaper, at least, considered the fight "famous" among its readers. The *Tribune* later memorialized the eleventh anniversary of "the important engagement with the Indians on the Bear River" in its pages. The results of the massacre were "the theme of praise from the press all over the Pacific Coast."[32]

Other than renaming Beaver Creek "Battle Creek" shortly after the massacre, about half a century would pass before Cache Valley citizens in the neighborhood of the battlefield would consider any kind of formal recognition of the site. An undated entry—but probably around 1914 or 1915 given the context—in a Franklin County history mentions the donation of half an acre of ground at the scene of the fight, "Where we hope to erect a monument in honor of the Soldiers who lost their lives."[33]

The Daughters of Utah Pioneers chronicled the lengthy process of their building of a monument at the site. Their account says the original idea for a monument came from an educator and the father-and-son editors of the local newspaper, perhaps as early as 1916.[34] A publicity campaign launched by the paper included an editorial which said that every summer drivers by the hundreds pass the place, unaware, "where a number of soldiers and hundreds of our dark skinned friends were slain."

But the suggested monument was not meant to honor all those killed. "We feel something is due the soldiers who came here and died that this country might not be troubled by marauding Indains."[35] The campaign drew a response from Be-shup, a son of Sagwitch who survived the massacre to be raised by a Mormon family as Frank Timbimboo Warner. "A monument to cruelty" is how he characterized the plan. For him, the shrine would stand in memory to "the many little innocent children that suffered death because they could not help themselves."[36]

Traveling at speed along the highway north and west of Preston, Idaho, as it crosses the Bear River bottoms, you could easily miss the Daughters of Utah Pioneers Battle of Bear River monument. Although easily overlooked, the monument was years in the making.

The women's organization started raising money in earnest about 1926 by subscription from area Mormon congregations. Efforts to obtain money from the government didn't pay off.

The memorial's design incorporated a nearly eight-foot-tall pylon of piled and mortared stone, and an invitation went out through the local Boy Scouts for rocks. More than 400 made their way into the shrine, from as far afield as Alaska and the Alleghenies, Niagara Falls and New Zealand. A bronze plaque, donated by the Utah Trails and Landmark Association, graced the face of the monument.[37]

160

"The Battle of Bear River was fought in this vicinity," the tablet read. About 500 Indians, "guilty of hostile attacks on emigrants and settlers," engaged 300 California Volunteers. Killed, according the account cast in bronze, were 250 to 300 Shoshoni and Bannock, "including about 90 combatant women and children." Bear Hunter and Lehi, along with Sagwitch, it said, "were reported killed." Also recounted were the numbers of dead and wounded soldiers, the burning of seventy lodges, the capture of 175 horses, and the recovery of "much stolen property."

Although there is no evidence of Bannock presence at the winter camp on the *Boa Ogoi* the day of the massacre, labeling the killed women and children "combatants" is questionable, and the claimed death of Sagwitch is incorrect, the information on the plaque essentially agreed with most reports of the massacre. Rather than celebratory in tone, the text seemed mostly neutral and impersonal.

"Next Monday representatives of two races—long separated—will meet to unveil a monument which will mark the last conflict between them in the state," the local newspaper reported August 31, 1932. The story downplayed the "battle at Battle Creek," calling it, surprisingly, a "small engagement" where "no particular heroism was displayed."[38]

Five to ten thousand people reportedly attended the dedication. Among them, several Shoshoni.[39] At least some of the Shoshoni were said to be reluctant participants. "The Washakie Settlement was ordered by their white bishop [local Mormon congregational leader] to attend this degrading ceremony in their full regalia"[40] according to one report. Photographed at the event were massacre survivor Yeager Timbimboo and his son Mornoni,[41] both residents of the Washakie settlement at the time. But rather than ceremonial Shoshoni clothing, they are dressed in the ceremonial garb of the white man—starched shirts and neckties.

Nevertheless, if tribal members found little to like about the 1932 commemoration, there would be little to change that view in the decades to come.

⁂

For twenty-one years the Daughters of Utah Pioneers Battle Creek marker stood silent sentinel beside the highway, with nothing to add to the words on its bronze plaque. In 1953, a second plaque was attached to the squat spire's opposite face. If the text of this description of events is any indication, local notions of what happened at the site—and what was worth remembering— had shifted.

"Pioneer Women" were now the focus. The words "Attacks by the Indians on peaceful inhabitants in this vicinity" rendered the cause of the engagement a simple, one-sided affair. "Scores of wounded and frozen soldiers were taken from the battlefield to the Latter Day Saint community of Franklin," it told. Then, in heroic prose, said, "Pioneer women, trained through trials and necessity of frontier living, accepted the responsibility of caring for the wounded." Succor extended to the Shoshoni, as well: "Two Indian women and three children, found alive after the encounter, were given homes in Franklin."

It is, in some sense, understandable that descendants of pioneer women would celebrate the role of their ancestors on a monument of their making. But still missing at the site was any memorial to the Shoshoni, or even acknowledgement that their memories of the fight might tell a different story.

The erection of government-built roadside historical markers added detail to the understanding of travelers who chanced to stop. "Bear River Battle" the original state sign read, in words prepared by the Idaho Historical Society. "California Volunteers trapped and wiped out the Cache Valley Shoshoni," who, "with a loss of over 400. . .met the greatest Indian disaster in the entire West." Later, "Battle" was replaced with "Massacre" on the sign's heading. And, instead of "a loss of over 400," the text was altered to say that "More than 400 Shoshoni occupied a winter camp" at the site. No reference is made to body count in the "military disaster unmatched in western history."

The most detailed of the roadside markers wasn't erected at the site at all. Some twenty miles away, just south of Franklin—and across the state line—Utah erected a large sign, flanked by heavy stone pillars and weighted down heavy with text.

The sign told of the "Battle of Bear River, Last of the major engagements between U.S. Troops and outlaw Indians in northern Utah." Raids, killings, and the murder of "several" miners were recounted. Connor and his troops made a difficult march— guided by Orrin Porter Rockwell—to the Indian camp "where the renegades had taken refuge among a tribe of friendly Indians not involved in the outrage." Bear Hunter and Lehi were reported killed, but not Sagwitch. He, "leader of the friendly tribe...escaped & later helped establish his people in their own settlement." A reference, most likely, to the destroyed community of Washakie. The marker has since been removed, probably owing to confusion it created concerning the location of the event it memorialized.

If a picture is worth a thousand words, a twelve-foot-long mural, five feet high, ought to have plenty to say. Gracing the wall of the Post Office in Preston, Idaho, is an oil-on-canvas painting, "The Battle of Bear River," by Edmond J. Fitzgerald. The artist, well known for his murals, has out-sized works in post offices in Oregon and Washington, as well in the White House in Washington, D. C.

Post office murals went up across the country in the 1930s and into the forties until World War II proved too great a distraction to government budgets and priorities. Other Idaho communities— Blackfoot, Buhl, Burley, Kellogg, and St. Anthony—also displayed paintings from the program. The Public Works Project that produced them shifted around through several agencies and departments from its inception in 1933 until its demise a decade later, under the Fine Arts Section of the Federal Works Agency.

Artists competed for the work and were chosen and supervised by the federal government. Designs were selected to "reflect the themes and styles of the American scene," to "strike a responsive chord with the general public." However, given the need to avoid upsetting local preferences and win government approval, the art "tended to pursue an inoffensive middle ground of style and content . . .producing limp platitudes rather than strong statements."[42]

So much for the old saw about a thousand words.

"The Battle of Bear River" captures daybreak in the river bottom, with the sun's first rays reflecting off mountaintops in the background. The painter uses artistic license to exaggerate the terrain, rendering the bluffs flanking the river plain as sheer, steep cliffs.

But artistic license runs amok in depicting the fight itself. While most of the actual fighting was said to have occurred at close quarters within a confined area in and around the Beaver Creek ravine in a tangle of brush and willows, the painting casts small skirmishes wide across an open, too-flat, too-broad river valley. The hundreds of Californians and Shoshoni present at the engagement are nowhere to be seen, instead represented—symbolically, perhaps—by only a few dozen fighters. Of the seventy-or-so lodges concentrated in the ravine, only a handful are visible, one brilliantly ablaze in the dim light of the winter morning, with an orange glow in the background suggesting the presence of other lodges afire.

Cold is evident in the mural, captured in the snow covering the ground—albeit a thin blanket—as well as in the blue-tinged blush of early morning light. But the Shoshoni, apparently, are unaware of or unaffected by the sub-freezing temperatures of the morning of January 29, 1863, as they are uniformly bare-chested, most clad only in loincloths. But their scant apparel cannot be attributed to a lack of preparation time—despite coming under attack while

Mural of battle painted in the 1930 for the Preston, Idaho Post Office is short on historical accuracy.

most of the village was asleep—as some of the Shoshoni fighters apparently found time to unpack and adorn themselves with headdresses of flowing rows of feathers. And, despite most of the actual fighting having occurred on the ground by dismounted cavalry troopers and unmounted Indians, the mural shows many of the combatants, both soldier and Shoshoni, horseback.

It would be unfair, of course, to expect a work of art to realistically depict a scene as complex and chaotic as the Bear River Massacre. Still, a painting paid for with public funds, resulting from a government project, and on public display in a government building might, at least, be expected to more authentically illustrate reality.

Perhaps it is all part of the tone of the times. "The strife and dark side of the Depression were not portrayed" in the murals spawned by the Section of Fine Arts, Federal Works Agency program. A happier view was the order of the day, so the works—including, it is supposed, "The Battle of Bear River" mural in the Preston, Idaho Post Office—were to depict "nostalgic and positive events of the American Scene."[43]

Upon arrival in Franklin the night of January 28, 1863, Colonel Patrick Edward Connor sought out a local guide to pilot his forces the last few remaining miles to the Shoshoni winter camp on the Bear River.

Two brothers, Edmund and Joseph Nelson, reluctantly agreed to carry out the task. Afterward, they sat on the bluffs and watched the fighting below. The day after, the two brothers revisited the site and took along a brother, William. Ninety-four years later, in June, 1959, a group of historians met William's son, Taylor Nelson, for a tour of the killing field. His father and uncles had given him the tour previously, for he told the group, "I believe I am the only living man who was conducted over this battlefield by two men who were eyewitnesses and saw the battlefield after the fighting was over."

Barely two weeks after showing the historians around, Taylor Nelson died.

Nelson's memories of what he learned of the fight, according to a published report of the timely tour, portrayed the settlers as "deeply shocked by Connor's brutal slaughter of Indians, a majority of them non-combatants and many of them known to be friendly." The article concludes with a statement that historians, even then, were aware—or becoming so—of the heinous nature of the military attack. The "worst offense" of most of the Shoshoni killed in the fight, was, according to the story, a desire "to live as and where their ancestors had lived for generations."[44]

Cache Valley's largest newspaper remembered the hundredth anniversary of the massacre with a guest column. A student at Idaho State College in Pocatello, Idaho, Lieutenant Colonel Edward J. Barta, wrote a master's thesis on the "battle" and, at the suggestion of his advisor, extracted the article for publication. Perhaps owing to loyalties stemming from his military affiliation, the thesis, and the resultant article, display a decidedly pro-army point of view.

Barta claims there were 600 Cache Valley Shoshoni in the camp, as well as Bannock Indians and "Bannock Creek Shoshoni" under Pocatello. The Indians were well armed, "many of them having rifles superior in quality to those of the soldiers." Women and children fought beside the men until the Indians "broke and ran," but few managed to escape and "the Indians as a fighting force [were] nearly wiped out." The surviving women and children, 160 of them, "were fed by the soldiers and allowed to depart." Sagwitch and Pocatello did not fight that day, as they had fled the camp the day before.

Barta credited the Shoshoni (and Bannock) with a tactic unique in Indian warfare, deliberately taking the defensive in a form of trench warfare. The tactic ultimately proved futile, however, and "The battle. . .effectively ended Indian depredations on a large scale in northern Utah and southeastern Idaho."[45] While much of what Barta wrote has since been displaced by more extensive studies, his may well have been the first in-depth research into the fight.

Interest in the Bear River Massacre took a decided turn for the better in the 1980s. No doubt Brigham D. Madsen's campaign to change the fight's designation from battle to massacre, with an important lecture on the subject in 1983—the text of which was widely distributed—played a role. The 1985 publication of his book *The Shoshoni Frontier and the Bear River Massacre* was likely instrumental. Not only did the book make an important contribution on its own, it also provided broader exposure for Mae Parry's account of Shoshoni memories of the bloodbath by appending her important "Massacre at Boa Ogoi" to the book.

Newell Hart's privately published comprehensive compilation of massacre documents, reports, accounts, and related material, released in 1982, made easily accessible much information previously scattered in archives and newspaper morgues and personal collections throughout the West.

167

A grass-roots crusade, organized as the Bear River-Battle Creek Monument Association under the direction of Preston, Idaho, resident Allie Hansen lobbied extensively with government officials and business leaders at all levels. The group explored a number of avenues for protecting the site, as well as conducting tours for thousands of visitors over the years.

Even the military's views shifted during the decade of the 1980s. To commemorate the 125th anniversary, a caravan of some ninety ROTC cadets from two Utah universities traveled to the location of the Shoshoni winter camp on the Bear River for a "staff walk." Rather than attempt to decipher battle tactics, geography, and terrain from written accounts and maps, the students hiked the bluffs and river bottom. Following the tracks of the California Volunteers, they imagined the Shoshoni lodges, eyeballed battle lines and strategies, visualized the carnage. Civil war re-enactors lectured the cadets on Civil War-era weapons, uniforms, and accoutrements.

The group also discussed the morality of the massacre. "Our point of view tends to be a bit slanted to that of the military," said the officer leading the expedition. "I wish there had been more of a dissenting opinion presented."[46] Even recognizing that differing opinions merit consideration was likely a big step for many in uniform. But the cadets took an even bigger step. A vote was taken to assess opinions on whether the engagement had been a battle. There was no need to count votes—the cadets unanimously labeled it a massacre.[47]

Intensified interest and the efforts among many, including historians, grassroots groups, members of the Northwestern Band of the Shoshone Nation, and civic leaders in Cache Valley, finally bore fruit.

In 1986, the joint legislatures of Utah and Idaho resolved to create a "Battle of Bear River Monument." The Shoshoni, unhappy with use of the word "Battle," threatened suit to force a shift in emphasis toward the Indian point of view. As a result of the dispute, elected officials in both states asked the federal government to provide a broader view, in the form of a study to investigate suitability of the site for national, rather than state, landmark status.

The result of the investigation by National Park Service historian Edwin C. Bearss and the National Park Service Advisory Board was an October 19, 1990 dedication ceremony celebrating official government recognition of the fight as a massacre, and designation of the site as a National Historic Landmark. The landmark encompassed some 1,600 acres of river bottom and land above the bluffs, including the most significant sites within its boundaries.

Bearss intended to address crowds at the ceremony, but when missed airline connections prevented his being there, Brigham Madsen was drafted on short notice to speak to the assembly.[48] Acknowledging it was "fitting at long last to recognize the Bear River Massacre by establishing it as a National Historic Landmark," he encouraged more action. "Before too many years have passed," he said, "the citizens of the area and the State and Federal Government should set aside this parcel of ground as a sacred and hallowed spot."[49] Yet another bronze plaque was unveiled on the Daughters of Utah Pioneers monument, this one leaving no doubt that what occurred on the site was a massacre.

Not everyone came away from the dedication pleased with the turn of events, it seems. Allie Hansen, president of the Bear River-Battle Creek Monument Association, had fought long and hard to win recognition and protection for the site, including traveling to San Francisco to testify at Department of Interior hearings. Conversations at the dedication ceremony prompted her to write Madsen a few days later. "According to the Indians, what my group has accomplished in the last four years, in no way will help heal this '127 year old wound.' Why is this the case?" she asked, knowing Madsen had more experience with the Shoshoni than most. "Can you help me understand why it won't? We had the greatest hope that it would help."

Madsen attributed the slight to "independent individualism" among some members of the band, and "the development of factions" that made agreement difficult. Any involvement of whites in Shoshoni affairs, Madsen said, "can lead to even greater opposition," due to "mistrust they have developed over the years toward White officials and citizens."[50]

Uncomfortable alliance though it may have been for some, whites and Indians would continue to work, if not side by side, then at least in the same direction, toward a goal of greater recognition of and protection for the massacre site. Their greatest advocates in the process, and the greatest stumbling blocks in their path, would come from within the federal government.

⁂

With National Historic Landmark designation in hand, the National Park Service attacked the massacre site with a vengeance. Federal personnel descended on Franklin County, Idaho to study, assess, evaluate, catalog, categorize, measure, map, plan, plat, and plot whether or not the site merited further protection as part of the national park system. The result was a one-hundred-sixty page book, *Final Resource Study and Environmental Assessment, Bear River Massacre Site*, released in 1997 by the United States Department of the Interior, National Park Service, and preceded by the 1995 release of a draft of the document.

Narrative, charts, graphs, illustrations, tables, and maps told the story of the massacre. The study outlines the history of the ownership of the site since, including maps showing who owned which parcels at the time of the study. Cultural resources, the natural environment, and socioeconomic conditions of the area were analyzed. Comparisons were drawn to similar sites and comparable events to place the massacre within historic context. No fewer than twenty-five meetings were accounted, from study groups of experts to consultations with Shoshoni leaders, to government officials and elected leaders, to landowners, to public meetings in various locations. Newsletters and interim reports were distributed to interested and affected parties.

The study determined the massacre met all criteria for federal protection, and that the significance of the event to American history merited recognition. The final study presented, without recommendation, five alternatives for the site, two of which present the feasibility of state and local governments managing the site, two of which would make the site part of the national park system.

Also assessed was the practicality of taking no action; maintaining status as a National Historic Landmark and relying on the goodwill of property owners to protect and preserve the site. No additional interpretative or informative material would be provided for visitors.

Alternative 1 outlined what might happen with minimal action, maintaining Historic Landmark status. Current land ownership would be preserved, but with certain preservation-related protections required through local ordinances. The existing roadside stop would be expanded to provide a basic, but more informative, more balanced story of what happened there January 29, 1863.

With protection as a State Historic Site, Alternative 2, conservation easements and state law would provide additional protection for the land, but current ownership and voluntary guidelines would still hold sway. More interpretive facilities would be added, including a visitor center and overlook on the bluffs above.

Alternative 3, designation as a National Historic Reserve, would include public ownership of the massacre field, and sites for multiple overlooks and interpretive centers. The rural nature of the surrounding environment would be protected through easements and agreements with landowners.

Maximum protection, interpretation, and restoration would occur with Alternative 4, the creation of a National Historic Site. More of the surrounding land would be acquired with public funds; private landowners would be restricted by conservation and scenic easements. Visitor and cultural centers, operated by the National Park Service, the Shoshoni, and local interpreters, would offer a detailed, balanced view of events. Overlooks, interpretive trails, and other facilities would encourage longer visits and lure visitors out of their cars.

Each alternative was examined in detail on its own and compared to the others for visitor experience, effect on the local economy and culture; acquisition, construction, and operational costs; and a host of other factors. Each was accompanied by a detailed map showing possible locations for facilities, boundaries, overlooks, and existing roads and landmarks.[51]

The study, which left no stone unturned, was turned over to Congress, as required by law, in March, 1997. And there it has sat, unmoving as stone, ever since.

Somewhere, in the deep recesses of the office of Larry Craig, Idaho's senior senator, the push to protect the Bear River Massacre site lost momentum and stalled out. The reasons the Senator has given for his inactivity are many and various. Brigham Madsen was told the government couldn't afford it.[52] Allie Hansen was told by Craig, "I'll become more interested if you can get your local people interested." But, she says, "We have done everything we know how to do on our own."[53]

Another support group, The Friends of the Native Americans of Northern Utah, established in 1999 and led by Kerry Brinkerhoff, at the time a National Park Service Ranger working at the Golden Spike National Historic Site, gathered signatures for a petition to urge Congress to action. In replying to the petition, Senator Craig told Brinkerhoff he had "worked with local groups, both supporters and opponents, to get further input from all interested parties." He then gave three reasons for not introducing legislation to designate the massacre field a National Historic Site.

First was a seemingly philosophical opposition to acquiring "private property to build massive federal sites." Second, a refusal to involve the National Park Service until "after the large backlog of current projects is resolved." His third reason the project was "stalled" was "because of concerns raised by tribal descendants."

The claim of "concerns raised by tribal descendants" surprised many in the Northwestern Band of the Shoshone Nation. A great-great-granddaughter of Sagwitch, Patty Timbimboo Madsen, was "mortified." Tribal Cultural Specialist at the time, she was in a position to know. Madsen herself, along with her extended family—which includes numerous descendants of both massacre survivors and victims, and represents a goodly portion of present-day tribal leaders and members—had worked with the park service for years, through every phase of the study process.

She was also curious to know how—and why—the site had fallen so low on the priority list, the "large backlog." Madsen reminded Brinkerhoff that the Sand Creek Massacre field, a likewise worthy site, had been studied, assessed, and declared a National Historic Site by Congress while the Bear River site languished. She credited Colorado Senator Ben Nighthorse Campbell for pressing action on Sand Creek—a marked contrast to Senator Craig's indifference or, perhaps, opposition to the Bear River Massacre National Historic Site.[54]

Another of Chief Sagwitch's progeny, Bruce Parry, executive director of the Northwestern Band of the Shoshone Nation, acknowledged that in the past some tribal members disagreed about how the massacre site should be recognized. Some wanted nothing to do with the National Park Service, fearing the Bear River Massacre would become yet another opportunity for whites to make money at the expense of American Indian history. "They were against everything."

But, Parry said, "All those guys have died."[55]

So too, it seemed, had the Bear River Massacre National Historic Site as a unit of the National Park Service.

⁂

Not content to wait out the stagnant pace of political and bureaucratic action in Washington, D.C., the Shoshoni continually sought other avenues for protecting the land where the bones of so many ancestors lay scattered and unsanctified.

So it was that in March, 2003, the tribe gained title to twenty-six of the 1,690 acres within the boundaries of the National Historic Landmark. While the acquired acreage represents but a tiny fraction of the massacre site, it lies at its heart, encompassing the area where many of the lodges stood and many of the Shoshoni fell.

Funding for the purchase was assembled from several donors, in cooperation with the Trust for Public Lands. Some 200 people gathered March 24 to commemorate the closing.

"We've waited many years for this day to happen," said Gwen Davis, Tribal Chairwoman. "Our dreams have become reality today."[56]

Bruce Parry, executive director, said, "It's nice to own your graveyard."[57]

Patty Timbimboo Madsen claimed shame over the unburied remains of her ancestors. "They're calling out for someone to help them, to send them on their way." Now her people owned the land, she said, and she could visit the site without feeling she "was intruding on the non-Indian space."[58]

Many other words were spoken by many others that day. But none echoed down the years like those of Shoshoni holy man Ricky Hasuse, who blessed the victims and the land in a native-language ceremony—the first and only rites for the tribe's dead since the slaughter at that place on the *Boa Ogoi* on January 29, 1863.[59]

Chapter Seven notes

1. "The Battle of Bear River, January 29, 1863" by Captain Melvin . Littig, U.S.A.; The Fort Douglas Museum of Military History, Fort Douglas, Utah, 1977
2. Madsen, Brigham D. *The Bannock of Idaho.* Moscow: University of Idaho Press, 1966, p. 111
3. Madsen, Brigham D. *The Shoshoni Frontier and the Bear River Massacre.* Salt Lake City: University of Utah Press, 1985, p. xv
4. Author interview with Brigham D. Madsen, March 10, 2006
5. *Deseret Morning News*, February 28, 2002
6. *Final Special Resource Study Environmental Assessment, Bear River Massacre Site, Idaho.* United States Department of Interior, National Park Service, 1996, p. 3
7. Schindler, Harold. "The Bear River Massacre: New Historical Evidence," *Utah Historical Quarterly*, Fall 1999, p. 302
8. Interview with Brigham D. Madsen, March 10, 2006
9. Hart, Newell. *The Bear River Massacre.* Preston: Cache Valley Newsletter Publishing Company, Second Printing 1983, pp. 165-184
10. Bagley, Will. "Bear River Massacre Continues to Haunt Utah History After 140 Years," *Salt Lake Tribune*, January 26, 2003
11. Description of John Vance Lauderdale Papers, Yale Collection of Western Americana, Yale University (Internet access, December 6, 2006)
12. Bigler, David L. *Forgotten Kingdom: The Mormon Theocracy in the American West, 1847-1896.* Logan: Utah State University Press, 1998, pp. 89-92
13. "Autobiographical Sketch of the Life of Richard John Moxey Bee", p. 29. Americana Collection, Harold B. Lee Library, Brigham Young University
14. Interview with Newel J. Cutler, Syracuse, Utah by Martin E. Seneca, Jr., August 11, 1967 (Duke No. 61, American Indian History Project, Western History Center, U of U). The Brigham D. Madsen Papers, Ms 671, Box 76, Manuscripts Division, J. Willard Marriott Library, University of Utah
15. "Biography of Hans Jasperson," pp. 3-4, and letter from Hans Jasperson to the Utah Legislature, January 25, 1913, in private collection of Merrill J. Nelson, West Valley City, Utah
16. Lehi Centennial Committee. *Lehi Centennial History, 1850-1950*, "Sylvanus Collett". Lehi: Free Press Publishing Co., 1950, pp. 237-239
17. Statement of Christian Garff to Benjamin Franklin Riter. "Collection of letters and documents concerning Jim Bridger, Cache Valley, and the Battle of Bear River," Utah State Historical Society
18. Simmonds A. J., "Looking Back." *Logan Herald Journal.* August 14, 1978
19. McPherson, Robert S. *Staff Ride Handbook for the Battle of Bear River—29 January 1863.* Riverton: Utah National Guard, 2000, pp. 76-79
20. "Henry Woonsook, Fort Hall, Idaho—A Historical Tale Told To Lorin Gaarder, February 29, 1968." The American Indian History Project Supported by Miss Doris Duke, Western History Center, University of Utah, Marriott Library Special Collections
21. Sweeten, Colen. "Moroni Timbimboo Interview," Provo: Charles Redd Center for Western Studies, Brigham Young University Oral History Project, 1970, p. 2
22. *Franklin County Citizen*, July 11, 1918
23. Leland Pubigee interview, "Northwestern Band of the Shoshone Nation" (video program) Norman: University of Oklahoma American Indian Institute in conjunction with Northwestern Band of the Shoshone Nation, Lewis-Clark State College Educational Technology Department, State of Idaho Department of Health and Welfare. 1992
24. Lila Jones interview, "Northwestern Band of the Shoshone Nation" (video program) Norman: University of Oklahoma American Indian Institute in conjunction with Northwestern Band of the Shoshone Nation, Lewis-Clark State College Educational Technology Department, State of Idaho Department of Health and Welfare. 1992
25. *Union Vedette*, January 28, 1864
26. *Union Vedette*, January 30, 1864
27. *Union Vedette*, February 1, 1864
28. *Union Vedette*, January 28, 1865
29. *Union Vedette*, January 29, 1867
30. *Montana Post*, February 9, 1867 (The Brigham D. Madsen Papers, J. Willard Marriott Library, University of Utah)

175

31. *Salt Lake Tribune*, September 20, 1872
32. *Salt Lake Tribune*, January 29, 1874
33. Danielsen, Marie, compiler. *The Trail Blazer: History of the Development of Southeastern Idaho*. Daughters of the Pioneers, 1930, p. 93
34. *Franklin County Citizen*, February 14, 1980, p. 5
35. *Franklin County Citizen*, December 7, 1916, quoted in *Franklin County Citizen*, August 31, 1932 (transcribed from copy in Newell Hart Papers, Merrill-Cazier Library Special Collections, Utah State University)
36. *Franklin County Citizen*, July 11, 1918
37. *Franklin County Citizen*, February 14 and 21, 1980
38. *Franklin County Citizen*, August 31, 1932 (transcribed from a copy in the Newell Hart Papers, Special Collections, Merrill-Cazier Library, Utah State University)
39. Hart, Newell, editor. *The Trail Blazer*. Updated edition, Preston: Cache Valley Newsletter Publishing Company, 1976 p. 161
40. Washines, Lorena, "Oral History Interview with Lee Neaman Concerning the Shoshone Indians" Merrill-Cazier Library Special Collections, Utah State University
41. Hart, Newell, editor. *The Trail Blazer*. Updated edition, Preston: Cache Valley Newsletter Publishing Company, 1976 p. 135
42. "Preston Post Office Mural" informational handout collected at United States Postal Service, Preston, Idaho, Post Office, September 22, 2006
43. "Preston Post Office Mural" informational handout collected at United States Postal Service, Preston, Idaho, Post Office, September 22, 2006
44. Hayward, Ira. "The Battle of Battle Creek," *SUP News*, (Sons of Utah Pioneers), November, 1959, p. 8-9
45. Nelson, Ray. "Thoughts and Things," *The Herald Journal*, Logan and Cache Valley, January 29, 1963
46. Daily Utah Chronicle, February 4, 1988
47. Madsen, Brigham D. *Against the Grain: Memoirs of a Western Historian*. Salt Lake City: Signature Books, 2002, p. 334
48. Madsen, Brigham D. *Against the Grain: Memoirs of a Western Historian*. Salt Lake City: Signature Books, 2002, p. 333
49. The Brigham D. Madsen Papers, Special Collections, Marriott Library, University of Utah
50. The Brigham D. Madsen Papers, Special Collections, Marriott Library, University of Utah
51. United States Department of the Interior, National Park Service. *Final Resource Study and Envirnomental Assessment, Bear River Massacre Site, 1997*, pp. x-160
52. Author interview with Brigham D. Madsen, March 10, 2006
53. *Salt Lake Tribune*, January 27, 2003
54. Brinkerhoff, Kerry. "No one hears the cries of those massacred 138 years ago or their descendants today," 2001 online posting, accessed January 17, 2003 at http://www.genealogical-institute.com/no_one_hears
55. *Salt Lake Tribune*, January 27, 2003
56. *Salt Lake Tribune*, March 25, 2003
57. *Salt Lake Tribune*, March 12, 2003
58. *Deseret News*, March 25, 2003
59. *Deseret News*, March 25, 2003

AFTERWORD

While protection and recognition of the Bear River Massacre site is as yet at a standstill in Washington owing to political prejudice, ambivalence, and apathy, the Northwestern Band of the Shoshone Nation refuses to sit still.

Travelers driving past the killing field today can follow a short asphalt road off the highway to a paved parking area atop the bluffs opposite the place the United States Army rode down to destroy the Shoshoni winter camp on the *Boa Ogoi*. Curved in a gentle arc along the escarpment is a series of interpretive signs. Illustrated and colorful, the placards explain the history of the Shoshoni and their use of the area, changes wrought by white settlement, events leading up to the massacre, and the chronology of the fight with key locations identified. The overlook, opened in September of 2006, was paid for by the Idaho Transportation Department.

But the Shoshoni are not satisfied, and work will continue. "It is their dream," a signboard headlined "The Earth Will Remember" says, "that one day the Warm Dance, which has not happened since the massacre, will be celebrated again on this sacred ground. Today, the Northwestern Band of the Shoshone Nation continues on in strength and hope."

Near the southern end of Cache Valley near Wellsville, Utah, The American West Heritage Center commemorates the past through a variety of exhibits, living history, and educational programs. In early 2008, the Center reported receiving grants from several donors to create a 2,000 square-foot museum exhibit in its Welcome Center to tell the story of the Bear River Massacre. The permanent exhibit "will be supplemented by a driving tour map that will guide visitors to the massacre site near Preston, Idaho." David Sidwell, program director at the American West Heritage Center, said, "As a museum and center for history in our area, our goal is to present important stories. The Bear River Massacre is not a pretty story, but it's an important story. It's a story that should be told."[1]

Afterword Notes

1. *Salt Lake Tribune*, February 19, 2008

BIBLIOGRAPHY

Books

Arrington, Leonard J. and Bitton, Davis. *The Mormon Experience.* Urbana and Chicago: University of Illinois Press, 1992

Bancroft, Hubert Howe. *History of Utah, 1540-1886, Volume XXVI.* San Francisco: The History Company, Publishers, 1889

Bigler, David L. *Forgotten Kingdom: The Mormon Theocracy in the American West, 1847-1896.* Logan: Utah State University Press, 1998

Brown, Dee. *Bury My Heart at Wounded Knee.* New York: Henry Holt and Company, 1970 (Owl Book edition, 1991)

Burton, Sir Richard F. *The City of the Saints.* Santa Barbara: The Narrative Press, 2003

Carter, Kate B., compiler. *Our Pioneer Heritage: Volume Six.* Salt Lake City: Daughters of the Utah Pioneers, 1963

Christensen, Scott R. *Sagwitch: Shoshone Chieftain, Mormon Elder, 1822-1887.* Logan: Utah State University Press, 1999

Danielsen, Marie, compiler. *The Trail Blazer: History of the Development of Southeastern Idaho.* Daughters of the Pioneers, 1930

DeVoto, Bernard, editor. *The Journals of Lewis and Clark.* Boston: Houghton Mifflin Company, 1953

Final Special Resource Study and Environmental Assessment, Bear River Massacre Site, Idaho. United States Department of Interior, National Park Service, 1996

Hance, Irma Watson, complier. *Johnston, Connor, and the Mormons: An Outline of Military History in Northern Utah.* Salt Lake City: privately published, 1962

Hart, Newell. *The Bear River Massacre.* Preston: Cache Valley Newsletter Publishing Company, Second Printing 1983

Hart, Newell, editor. *The Trail Blazer.* Updated edition, Preston: Cache Valley Newsletter Publishing Company, 1976

Hoig, Stan. *The Sand Creek Massacre.* Norman: University of Oklahoma Press, 1961

Holzapfel, Richard Neitzel. *Utah: A Journey of Discovery*. Salt Lake City: Gibbs Smith, Publisher, 1999

Josephy, Alvin M., Jr. *The Civil War in the American West*. New York: Vintage Books, 1993

Kreitzer, Matthew E., editor. *The Washakie Letters of Willie Ottogary*. Logan: Utah State University Press, 2000

Lehi Centennial Committee. *Lehi Centennial History, 1850-1950*, "Sylvanus Collett." Lehi: Free Press Publishing Co., 1950

LeSueur, Stephen C. *The 1838 Mormon War in Missouri*. Columbia: University of Missouri Press, 1987

Ludlow, Daniel H., Editor. *Encyclopedia of Mormonism*. New York: Macmillan Publishing Company, 1992

Madsen, Brigham D. *Against the Grain: Memoirs of a Western Historian*. Salt Lake City: Signature Books, 2002

Madsen, Brigham D. *The Bannock of Idaho*. Moscow: University of Idaho Press, 1966

Madsen, Brigham D. *Chief Pocatello*. Moscow: University of Idaho Press, 1999

Madsen, Brigham D. *Corinne: The Gentile Capital of Utah*. Salt Lake City: Utah State Historical Society, 1980

Madsen Brigham D. *Glory Hunter: A Biography of Patrick Edward Connor*. Salt Lake City: University of Utah Press, 1990

Madsen, Brigham D. *The Lemhi: Sacajawea's People*. Caldwell: Caxton Printers, Ltd., 1990

Madsen, Brigham D. *The Northern Shoshoni*. Caldwell: Caxton Printers, 1980

Madsen, Brigham D. *The Shoshoni Frontier and the Bear River Massacre*. Salt Lake City: University of Utah Press, 1985

McPherson. Robert S. *Staff Ride Handbook for the Battle of Bear River— 29 January 1863*. Riverton: Utah National Guard

Moorman, Donald R. and Sessions, Gene A. *Camp Floyd and the Mormons: The Utah War*. Salt Lake City: University of Utah Press, 1992

Nevin, David. *The Old West: The Soldiers*. New York: Time-Life Books, 1973

Parry, Mae. "Early History" in *Coyote Steals Fire: A Shoshone Tale*. Retold and Illustrated by The Northwestern Band of the Shoshone Nation. Logan: Utah State University Press, 2005

Parry, Mae. "Massacre at Boa Ogoi" in Madsen, Brigham D. *The Shoshoni Frontier and Bear River Massacre*. Salt Lake City: University of Utah Press, Appendix B

Parry, Mae. "The Northwestern Shoshone" in *A History of Utah's American Indians*. Edited by Cuch, Forrest S. Salt Lake City: Utah State Division of Indian Affairs / Utah State Division of History, 2000

Peterson, F. Ross. *A History of Cache County*. Salt Lake City: Utah State Historical Society and Cache County Council, 1997

Quinn, D. Michael. *The Mormon Hierarchy: Origins of Power*. Salt Lake City: Signature Books, 1994

Roberts, B.H., editor. *History of the Church of Jesus Christ of Latter-day Saints*, "Propositions of the Mob." Salt Lake City: Church of Jesus Christ of Latter-day Saints, 1957

Roberts, Brigham H. *A Comprehensive History of the Church of Jesus Christ of Latter-day Saints* Volume 4. Salt Lake City: Deseret News Press, 1930

Schindler, Harold. *Orrin Porter Rockwell: Man of God/Son of Thunder*. Salt Lake City: University of Utah Press, Second Edition, 1983

Smith, Joseph. *The Doctrine and Covenants of the Church of Jesus Christ of Latter-day Saints*. Salt Lake City: The Church of Jesus Christ of Latter-day Saints, 1989

Smith, Joseph. *History of the Church Vol. 5*. Salt Lake City: Deseret Book Company, 1948

Steward, Julian H. *Basin-Plateau Aboriginal Sociopolitical Groups*. Washington: United States Government Printing Office, 1938 (reprint, 1997, The University of Utah Press, Salt Lake City)

Thayer, Thomas N. and Murphy, Shar L. *Discovering Tomorrow Through Yesterday: Idaho History*. Billings: Northwest Speaks, 2001

Unruh, John David. *The Plains Across: The Overland Emigrants and the Trans-Mississippi West, 1840-1860*. Urbana: University of Illinois Press, 1979

Wheeler, Keith. *The Old West: The Scouts*. Alexandria: Time-Life Books, 1978

Young, Virgil M. *The Story of Idaho*. Moscow: University Press of Idaho, 1977

Newspapers

Daily Utah Chronicle, University of Utah, February 4, 1988

Denver Republican, Denver, May 18, 1890

Deseret News, Salt Lake City, August 20, 1862

Deseret News, Salt Lake City, September 10, 1862

Deseret News, Salt Lake City, September 24, 1862

Deseret News, Salt Lake City, October 15, 1862

Deseret News, Salt Lake City, November 19, 1862

Deseret News, Salt Lake City, December 10, 1862

Deseret News, Salt Lake City, December 17, 1862

Deseret News, Salt Lake City, December 24, 1862

Deseret News, Salt Lake City, December 31, 1862

Deseret News, Salt Lake City, January 7, 1863

Deseret News, Salt Lake City, January 14, 1863

Deseret News, Salt lake City, January 21, 1863

Deseret News, Salt Lake City, January 28, 1863

Deseret News, Salt Lake City, February 4, 1863

Deseret News, Salt Lake City, February 11, 1863

Deseret News, Salt Lake City, May 20, 1868

Deseret News, Salt Lake City, September 1, 1875

Deseret Morning News, Salt Lake City, February 28, 2002

Deseret Morning News, Salt Lake City, March 25, 2003

Franklin County Citizen, Preston, Idaho, July 11, 1918

Franklin County Citizen, Preston, Idaho, August 31, 1932

Franklin County Citizen, Preston, Idaho, February 14, 1980

Franklin County Citizen, Preston, Idaho, February 21, 1980

Montana Post, February 9, 1867

New York Times, New York, February 25, 1863

Salt Lake Tribune, Salt Lake City, September 20, 1872

Salt Lake Tribune, Salt Lake City, January 29, 1874

Salt Lake Tribune, Salt Lake City, January 27, 2003

Salt Lake Tribune, Salt Lake City, March 12, 2003

Salt Lake Tribune, Salt Lake City, March 25, 2003

Salt Lake Tribune, Salt Lake City, February 19, 2008

Union Vedette, Salt Lake City, January 28, 1864

Union Vedette, Salt Lake City, January 30, 1864

Union Vedette, Salt Lake City, February 1, 1864

Union Vedette, Salt Lake City, August 31, 1864,

Union Vedette, Salt Lake City, October 27, 1864

Union Vedette, Salt Lake City, January 28, 1865

Union Vedette, Salt Lake City, January 29, 1867

Valley Tan, Salt Lake City, August 3, 1859

Valley Tan, Salt Lake City, September 7, 1859

Warsaw Signal. Warsaw, Illinois, July 21, 1841

Newspaper Columns and Magazine Articles

Bagley, Will. "Bear River Massacre Continues to Haunt Utah History After 140 Years," *Salt Lake Tribune*, January 26, 2003

Hayward, Ira. "The Battle of Battle Creek," *SUP News*, (Sons of Utah Pioneers), November, 1959

Nelson, Ray. "Thoughts and Things," *The Herald Journal*, Logan and Cache Valley, January 29, 1963

Schindler, Harold. "The Bear River Massacre: New Historical Evidence," *Utah Historical Quarterly,* Volume 67, Number 4, Fall 1999

Simmonds, A.J. "Looking Back: A first-hand account of the Battle of Bear River," *The Herald Journal*, Logan, Utah, April 9, 1979

Simmonds A. J., "Looking Back." *The Herald Journal,* Logan, Utah, August 14, 1978

Simmonds, A.J. "Looking Back: A reminiscence of the Battle of Bear River," *The Herald Journal/Valley*, Logan, Utah, August 20, 1979

Internet

California State Military Department, "The California Military Museum." Information "Extracted from *Records of California Men in the War of the Rebellion, 1861 To 1867*." Record located on the Internet, http://www.militarymuseum.org/2dCavVC.html, February 20, 2006

"Fort Ruby, Ruby Valley, Nevada," White Pine County Historical Society. Record located on the Internet, http://www.webpanda.com/white_pine_county/historical_society/ft_ruby.htm, February 19, 2003

Link, Paul K. and Phoenix, E. Chilton. *Rocks, Rails, and Trails.* Pocatello: Idaho Museum of Natural History, 1994, p. 47, Record located on the Internet, http://imnh.isu.edu/digitalatlas/geog/rrt/part3/chp6/47.htm, July 23, 2006)

Description of John Vance Lauderdale Papers, Yale Collection of Western Americana, Yale University (Internet access, December 6, 2006)

Brinkerhoff, Kerry. "No one hears the cries of those massacred 138 years ago or their descendants today," (2001), located on the Internet at http://www.genealogical-institute.com/no_one_hears, January 17, 2003

Oral Histories

Seneca, Martin E., Jr. "Interview with Newel J. Cutler, Syracuse, Utah, August 11, 1967" (Duke No. 61, American Indian History Project, Western History Center, U of U). The Brigham D. Madsen Papers, Ms 671, Box 76, Manuscripts Division, J. Willard Marriott Library, University of Utah

Sweeten, Colen. "Moroni Timbimboo Interview," Provo: Charles Redd Center for Western Studies, Brigham Young University Oral History Project, 1970

Washines, Lorena. "Oral History Interview with Lee Neaman" Logan: Utah State University, 1979. Special Collections, Utah State University, Merrill-Cazier Library, PAM C 109

Woonsock, Henry. "A Historical Tale Told To Lorin Gaarder, February 29, 1968," University of Utah, Western History Center, American Indian History Project, Doris Duke Number 352

Video Program

"Northwestern Band of the Shoshone Nation," Norman: University of Oklahoma American Indian Institute in conjunction with Northwestern Band of the Shoshone Nation, Lewis-Clark State College Educational Technology Department, State of Idaho Department of Health and Welfare. 1992

Interviews

Personal interviews with Brigham D. Madsen, March 3 and 10, 2006

Personal interview with Patty Timbimboo Madsen, secretary of the Northwestern Band of the Shoshone Nation, Brigham City, Utah, March 31, 2006

Fragments and Miscellaneous

"Autobiographical Sketch of the Life of Richard John Moxey Bee", p. 29. Americana Collection, Harold B. Lee Library, Brigham Young University

Littig, Melvin, Captain, U.S.A. "The Battle of Bear River, January 29, 1863," The Fort Douglas Museum of Military History, Fort Douglas, Utah, 1977

Letter from Mae Timbimboo Parry to Mr. And Mrs. Newell Hart, April 8, 1976. Newell Hart Papers, Mss 3, Box 29; Marie Eccles-Caine Archive of Intermountain Americana, Merrill-Cazier Library, Utah State University.

"Preston Post Office Mural" informational handout collected at United States Postal Service, Preston, Idaho, Post Office, September 22, 2006

Ricks, Joel. "Memories of Early Days in Cache County" From experiences of Margaret McNiel Ballard, "We arrived in Logan October 27th, 1859," p. 16, The Brigham D. Madsen Papers, Ms 671, Box 73, folder 1, Manuscripts Division, J. Willard Marriott Library, University of Utah

Statement of Christian Garff to Benjamin Franklin Riter. "Collection of letters and documents concerning Jim Bridger, Cache Valley, and the Battle of Bear River," Utah State Historical Society

Utah and the Civil War. Compiled and edited by Margaret M. Fisher. Salt Lake City: Deseret Book, 1929 (From The Brigham D. Madsen Papers, Ms 671, Box 73, folder 9. Manuscripts Division, J. Willard Marriott Library, University of Utah)

THE AUTHOR

Photograph by Chris Carr

A lifelong student of the culture and history of the West, Rod Miller writes nonfiction, fiction, and poetry on the subject. *Massacre at Bear River: First, Worst, Forgotten* is his third book.

Born and raised in Utah, Miller has lived most of his life on the eastern rim of the Great Basin, spent a few years on its western rim in Nevada, and also lived for a time on Idaho's Snake River Plain. He's a member of Western Writers of America.

INDEX

INDEX

Other titles about
the West
from

Caxton Press

Massacre Along the Medicine Road
The Indian War of 1864 in Nebraska
by Ronald Becher
ISBN 0-87004-289-7, 500 pages, cloth, $32.95
ISBN 0-87004-387-0, 500 pages, paper, $22.95

A Dirty, Wicked Town
Tales of 19th Century Omaha
by David Bristow
ISBN 0-87004-398-6, 320 pages, paper, $16.95

The Deadliest Indian War in the West
The Snake Conflict 1864-1868
by Gregory Michno
ISBN 0-87004-460-1, 450 pages, paper, $18.95

Necktie Parties
Legal Executions in Oregon, 1851 - 1905
by Diane Goeres-Gardner
ISBN 0-87004-446-x, 375 pages, paper, $16.95

A Fate Worse Than Death
Indian Captivities in the West, 1830-1885
by W. Gregory and Susan Michno
ISBN 0-87004-451-9, 512 pages, hardcover, $24.95

For a free catalog of Caxton titles write to:

Caxton Press
312 Main Street
Caldwell, Idaho 83605-3299

or

Visit our Internet web site:

www.caxtonpress.com

Caxton Press is a division of THE CAXTON PRINTERS, Ltd.